4

Second Edition

Grade

Jacob's Ladder

Reading Comprehension Program

4

Student Workbook Nonfiction

Contributing Editors:
Joyce VanTassel-Baska,
Tamra Stambaugh,
Kimberley L. Chandler

Contributing Authors:
Heather French,
Paula Ginsburgh,
Tamra Stambaugh,
Joyce VanTassel-Baska

William & Mary
School of Education

CENTER FOR GIFTED EDUCATION

William & Mary
School of Education
Center for Gifted Education
P.O. Box 8795
Williamsburg, VA 23187

First published in 2017 by Prufrock Press Inc.

Published 2021 by Routledge
605 Third Avenue, New York, NY 10017
2 Park Square, Milton Park, Abingdon, Oxon OX14 4RN

Routledge is an imprint of the Taylor & Francis Group, an informa business

Edited by Lacy Compton

Cover and layout design by Raquel Trevino

ISBN-13: 978-1-61821-735-6

Routledge
Taylor & Francis Group

NEW YORK AND LONDON

Table of Contents

The American Revolutionary War

In 1765, Americans still considered themselves loyal subjects to the British crown. Great Britain had just finished the Seven Years War with France, during which the Americans helped the British defeat the French on American soil. After the war ended, Great Britain was looking for a way to help pay for the war. Because part of the reason they went to war with France was to protect their colonies in America, the British government decided to pay for the war through taxing Americans. The taxes implemented by the British government were not necessarily high. However, Americans were upset that they were not consulted about the new taxes. The Americans felt it was illegal, or at the very least not fair, to tax them without giving them proper representation within the British parliament. The statement "No taxation without representation" became a well-known phrase during the American Revolutionary War.

The first direct tax against the colonies was the Stamp Act in 1765. The Stamp Act declared that all official documents, newspapers, almanacs, pamphlets, and even playing cards must have official stamps on them. If they did not have stamps, which Americans must buy from Britain, then fines would be charged. Later acts further restricted the activities of Americans. The Currency Act prohibited Americans from printing their own paper money, which hindered trade among the colonies. The Quartering Act mandated that American colonists house British soldiers in their homes, which invaded the colonists' privacy. Colonists began voicing their protests against these taxes and acts. In 1770, the Boston Massacre occurred in Massachusetts. In protest of the Stamp Act and the Tea Act, colonists dumped tea bricks from British ships into Boston Harbor, in what is now known as the Boston Tea Party. During this protest, five Americans were killed.

Because of incidents like this one, as well as philosophical differences between England and the colonies, and America's desire for independence, the American Revolutionary War, also known as the American War of Independence, began in 1775.

In 1776, representatives from each of the 13 colonies met in Philadelphia where they unanimously signed the Declaration of Independence, thereby forming the United States of America. In 1778, the colonists formed an alliance with France. The French helped by sending money, munitions, and troops. These contributions from France helped level the playing field in

the war against Britain. However, the Americans were fighting against a monarchy for the right to establish a democracy. Even though France was helping them win their independence, Americans did not view France as a role model.

During the war, only 1/3 of the colonists, known as Patriots, supported war with Britain, 1/3 of colonists, known as Loyalists, remained loyal to Britain, and 1/3 of colonists remained neutral. However, throughout the war, the Patriots maintained control over 80%–90% of the land. The British were able to capture only a few coastal cities, which they gained through their strong Navy presence.

At the Battle at Saratoga in 1777, one of Britain's main armies was captured, the beginning of the end for the British. In 1781, the British army surrendered at the Battle of Yorktown. This surrender led to the signing of the Treaty of Paris for peace in 1783.

THE AMERICAN REVOLUTIONARY WAR

Main Idea, Theme, or Concept

C3 Concept: What concept represents why the American Revolutionary War was fought? State your answer in five words or less.

_____

_____

_____

Inference

C2 What inferences can be made about the French becoming allies with the Americans during the American Revolutionary War? Justify your answer.

_____

_____

_____

_____

Literary Elements

C1 Choose to be a Patriot, a Loyalist, or a neutral colonist. Describe your character's point of view regarding the war. Support your answer with details.

_____

_____

_____

_____

_____

_____

_____

_____

Creative Synthesis

D3   Write a letter to your family about the American Revolutionary
War from the point of view of a colonist, a British soldier, or a
French soldier. Be sure to include enough details for the recipient
of your letter to understand the war from your point of view.

_____

_____

_____

_____

_____

_____

_____

_____

Summarizing

D2   In three sentences or fewer, summarize the cause(s) of the
American Revolutionary War.

_____

_____

_____

_____

Paraphrasing

D1   In your own words, rewrite the following statements:

"No taxation without representation."

_____

"Even though France was helping them win their independence,
Americans did not view France as a role model."

_____

_____

The Exploration of Space

The exploration of space gives scientists the opportunity to learn about the sun, stars, and planets. Some space exploration involves scientists called *astronauts* traveling into space. Astronauts use spacecraft, such as space shuttles, to travel beyond the Earth's atmosphere into outer space, which begins about 60 miles above sea level. While in outer space, astronauts explore their surroundings with various tools, such as safety tethering systems to keep their spacesuits attached to the spacecraft (and smaller tethers to attach their tools to their spacesuits). Astronauts might also wear a SAFER or Simplified Aid for EVA Rescue (EVA stands for extravehicular activity, another term for spacewalk). A SAFER is like a backpack that uses small jet thrusters to allow an astronaut to move in space. Other space exploration does not require astronauts but instead uses spacecraft with robots or other mechanical devices, such as satellites, to gather information.

In order for spacecraft, manned or unmanned, to travel into outer space, they must first overcome the pull of Earth's gravity. The heavier an object, the more power is required to break the Earth's gravitational pull. As you can imagine, it takes a tremendous amount of power to launch a space shuttle. These large spacecraft require booster rockets full of fuel to launch them. The boosters burn the fuel that gives off gas bursts that push the spacecraft into the air. The spacecraft eventually reaches a height where the Earth's gravitational pull no longer affects it. Once it passes this point, the shuttle only needs to fire rockets to increase its speed or to change directions.

When a spacecraft is ready to return to Earth, it must first slow down. Once it reenters the atmosphere, it slows down considerably and begins falling toward Earth. The spacecraft deploys, or puts into action, parachutes that further slow down its descent. Spacecraft like space shuttles land on runways just like airplanes. Some of the earlier U.S. spacecraft "splashed down" in the ocean where the astronauts were picked up by boats.

On October 4, 1957, the Soviet Union launched Sputnik, a satellite that orbited Earth, and space exploration officially began. Years later, on April 12, 1961, Yuri A. Gagarin, a Soviet cosmonaut, became the first person to travel to space. In December 1968, the U.S. took the first trip to the moon in

the spacecraft Apollo 8, orbiting the moon 10 times before returning to Earth. Less than a year later, the American astronaut Neil Armstrong became the first person to walk on the moon on July 20, 1969. As Armstrong placed the American flag on the moon, he said, "That's one small step for a man, one giant leap for mankind."

Since this historic landing on the moon, astronauts have continued to explore space by traveling there and by studying the data collected by satellites and other unmanned spacecraft. Through space exploration, astronauts and scientists have learned and continue to learn much about the universe beyond Earth.

THE EXPLORATION OF SPACE

Consequences and Implications

A3 What are the implications of space exploration? Support your answer.

_____

_____

_____

_____

_____

_____

_____

Cause and Effect

A2 What is the effect of the Earth's gravitational pull on spacecraft during launch? During reentry? Support your answer with evidence from the text.

_____

_____

_____

_____

_____

Sequencing

A1 In the space below, create a timeline of the history of space exploration as presented in the text.

Creative Synthesis

D3 Imagine you are an astronaut on the Apollo 8 spacecraft. Write a letter home describing the experience. Be sure to include plenty of details so the recipient of your letter feels like he or she was there with you.

_____

_____

_____

_____

_____

_____

_____

Summarizing

D2 In three sentences or fewer, describe the different ways scientists and astronauts explore space.

_____

_____

_____

_____

_____

_____

Paraphrasing

D1 In your own words, explain what Neil Armstrong meant when he said, "That's one small step for a man, one giant leap for mankind."

_____

_____

_____

_____

_____

_____

Graphic Ice Cream

Tim and Lauren, the owners of Crema, an ice cream shop in Raleigh, NC, surveyed their customers about their favorite ice cream flavors, gathered information about the number of customers on each day of the week, and asked their employees to keep track of how they spend their work hours. They then used different kinds of graphs to represent these data.

Over the period of one month, the Crema owners asked their customers to choose their favorite flavors from a list including chocolate, vanilla, strawberry, banana toffee, strawberry cheesecake, blueberry almond, chocolate raspberry, coffee almond, peach pecan, and caramel pecan. The results are presented in Table 1.

Table 1

Customers' Favorite Flavors

Ice Cream Flavor	Number of Customers' Favorite Flavor
Chocolate	120
Vanilla	65
Strawberry	85
Banana Toffee	190
Strawberry Cheesecake	275
Blueberry Almond	135
Chocolate Raspberry	200
Coffee Almond	95
Peach Pecan	150
Caramel Pecan	75

Tim and Lauren then decided to graph the data they had gathered from their customers. They chose to graph the favorite flavors on a bar graph. A bar graph shows the relationships between groups. On a bar graph, one bar is not affected by another. Bar graphs are a good way to show large differences in results from surveys. They also are excellent tools for determining trends. By using a bar graph to represent the data about customers' favorite flavors, Lauren and Tim will be better able to plan their purchases of ingredients. They will know which ingredients will be used more quickly based on the flavor preferences. The bar graph of Crema customers' favorite flavors is presented in Figure 1.

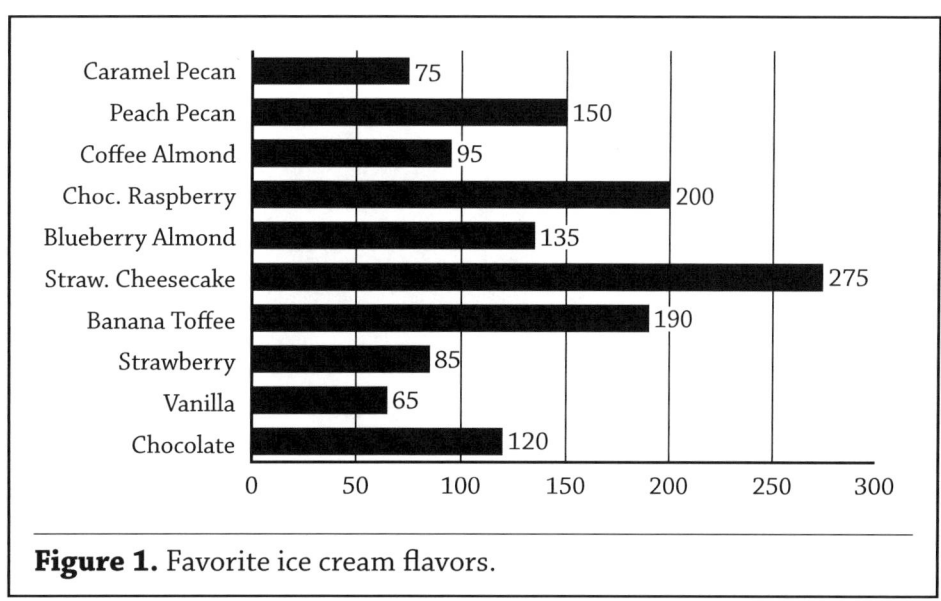

Figure 1. Favorite ice cream flavors.

After realizing how data can help them run their business more efficiently, Tim and Lauren decided to keep track of the number of customers coming to Crema on each day of the week. They were especially interested in Saturday and Sunday. They often wondered if they made or lost money by being open on the weekend. The results of their tracking are presented in Table 2.

Table 2

Number of Customers by Day

Day of the Week	Number of Customers
Monday	95
Tuesday	105
Wednesday	165
Thursday	210
Friday	275
Saturday	150
Sunday	45

Because the bar graph was helpful with comparing favorite flavors, the Crema owners decided to graph these data about customer attendance, too. However, instead of a bar graph, they chose to use a line graph. Line graphs track continuing data where one point is affected by another. With line graphs, there are points on a graph with x- and y-axis coordinates. Points are then joined by a line. Line graphs often are used to track rainfall, the average daily temperature, or, in the case of Crema, the daily number of customers. The line graph they used is presented in Figure 2.

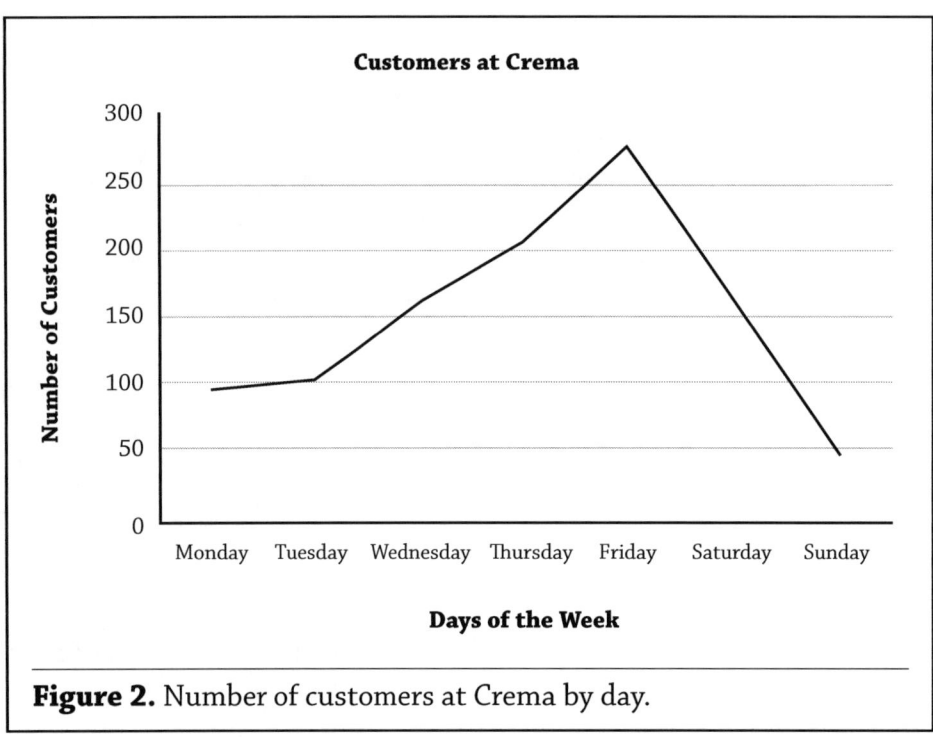

Figure 2. Number of customers at Crema by day.

Tim and Lauren analyzed the data to determine on what days they were most profitable. As they were thinking about money, they wondered how productive their employees were. They decided to ask their employees to keep track of how they spent their work hours. The results of this tracking are presented in Table 3.

Table 3

How Crema Employees Spend a Total Work Day (12 Hours)

Chore	Hours	Percentage of Work Day
Preparing Store to Open	1	8%
Taking Orders	3.5	30%
Preparing Orders	5	42%
Completing Transactions	1	8%
Reconciling Register	.5	4%
Closing	1	8%

The owners of Crema decided to use a circle, or pie, graph to display the data gathered from their employees. Pie graphs are particularly helpful when looking at how a part relates to a whole. In this case, Tim and Lauren wanted to see how the time spent on each chore related to the work day as a whole. The pie chart is presented in Figure 3.

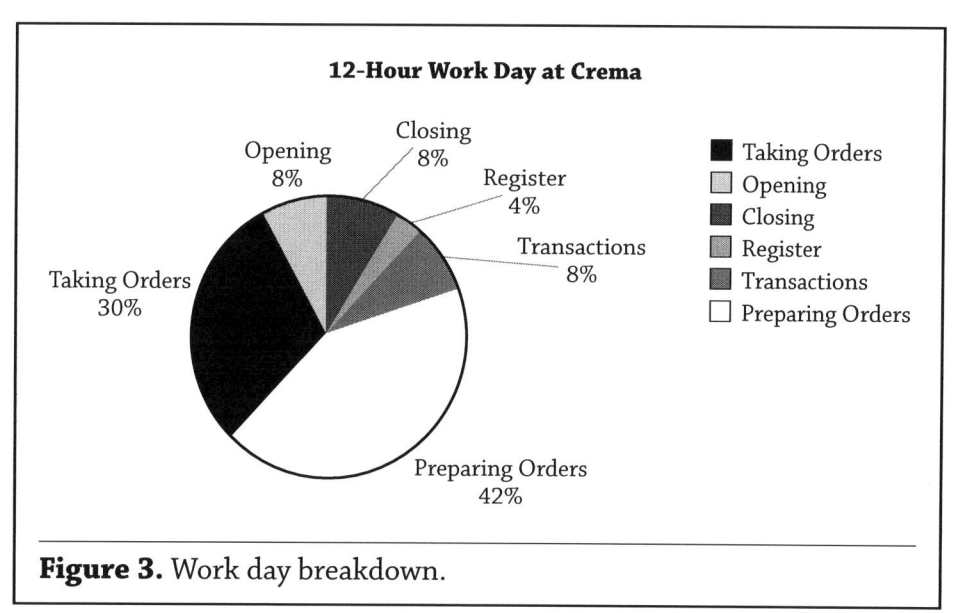

Figure 3. Work day breakdown.

GRAPHIC ICE CREAM

Generalizations

B3 Write at least three generalizations about using graphs to represent data.

_____

_____

_____

_____

Classifications

B2 Look at your list of details. Classify your list into the categories of bar, line, or pie graphs based on which type of graph would be most appropriate for each type of data. Use the definitions from the text to make your classification decisions.

_____

_____

_____

_____

_____

Details

B1 List 15–20 different kinds of data that are often gathered or that could be gathered.

_____

_____

_____

_____

_____

_____

_____

_____

Main Idea, Theme, or Concept

C3   Main Idea: Why did the author title this selection "Graphic Ice Cream"? Use evidence from the text to support your answer.

_____

_____

_____

_____

_____

Inference

C2   What inferences can you draw based on:
- the data and graph about customers' favorite flavors?
- the data and graph about daily customer counts?
- the data and graph about the use of employees' work hours?

_____

_____

_____

_____

_____

_____

_____

Literary Elements

C1   How would you characterize the owners of Crema? Using details from the text to support your answer, describe the kind of business owners they are.

_____

_____

_____

_____

_____

_____

_____

_____

The Great Depression

The Great Depression began in the United States with the stock market crash of 1929. The Depression quickly spread throughout Europe and then the rest of the world.

Economists are divided over what caused the Great Depression. Some believe that at the end of the post-World War I building boom, consumer goods were flooding the market. The supply of goods was far exceeding demand, which caused the economic system to collapse. Others believe that it was a simple case of too many banks playing the stock market with depositors' money. A third theory contends that the Depression deepened because so many people were carrying debt before the crash, and when the crash occurred they simply stopped spending money, which crippled the capitalist market. Another theory blames the severity of the Depression on the extreme drought that struck the Midwest agricultural business during the summer of 1930. Finally, a fifth theory states that it was the collapse of foreign banks that took with it a large amount of U.S. wealth and destroyed the prospect of world trade that caused the Depression to become a Great Depression.

Regardless of the cause, the Great Depression was one of the saddest periods in U.S. history. During this time period from 1929 to 1941, Americans endured much hardship. In the Midwest, farmers experienced an intense drought that earned this agricultural area the name "Dust Bowl." During the summer of 1930, many Midwest farmers were forced to leave their lands because of dust storms that blew much of the soil away. The dust storms were caused by a failure to rotate crops and the exposure of soil by the removal of grass through plowing. With the drought, the soil dried out, became dust, and then blew away in black clouds. Much of the soil was lost in the Atlantic Ocean as it blew eastward. Many people in the Midwest suffered from dust pneumonia and malnutrition.

In other areas of the country, conditions were not any better. Unemployment rose from 5 million people without jobs in 1930 to 11 million people without jobs in 1931. A staggering 25% of Americans were unemployed. Many people lost their homes. Sadly, 20% of children were hungry and did not have proper clothing or houses. Many schools closed because they could not afford to stay open. Of young people between the ages of 16 and 24, 40% of them were neither in school nor working. Children wrote letters to the First Lady, Eleanor Roosevelt, begging her to help them find food, clothing, and shelter.

After his inauguration in 1933, President Franklin D. Roosevelt passed the New Deal legislation. The New Deal restructured the economy and increased government spending to stimulate demand within the market, create jobs, and provide relief for the poor and unemployed. However, in 1937, the American economy took another nosedive that further deepened the Great Depression. During the period of the Depression, most countries experienced political upheaval that allowed dictators like Hitler, Stalin, and Mussolini to rise to power, leading to the beginning of World War II in 1939.

Supplying materials and resources for troops to protect the world against Nazi Germany stimulated economies in Europe from 1937–1939, pulling these nations out of depression. In the U.S., jobs increased, people worked overtime to make up for lost wages, and Americans agreed to rations for the first time in support of the war effort. The President pushed for a large quantity of war supplies no matter what it cost the government. In the United States, the Great Depression ended in 1941 when America entered World War II.

THE GREAT DEPRESSION

Consequences and Implications

A3 What were the consequences of the Great Depression for children? Justify your answer with supporting details.

_____

_____

_____

Cause and Effect

A2 What caused the end of the Great Depression in Europe? In America? Support your answer.

_____

_____

_____

_____

_____

_____

_____

Sequencing

A1 List, in order, the events of the Great Depression as discussed in the text.

_____

_____

_____

_____

_____

_____

_____

_____

Generalizations

B3 Write at least three generalizations about your life today compared
to the life of a child during the Great Depression.

_____

_____

_____

_____

Classifications

B2 Study your list. Classify your details into categories. You may not
have a "miscellaneous" or "other" category.

_____

_____

_____

_____

_____

_____

_____

_____

Details

B1 List at least 25 things and/or privileges that you have today that
you would not have had growing up during the Great Depression.

_____

_____

_____

_____

_____

_____

_____

_____

_____

_____

It's Electric!

How much do you know about electricity? Electricity refers to the movement of charged particles within atoms. There are two kinds of charged particles: Electrons have a negative charge, and protons have a positive charge. Electrons are constantly orbiting the nucleus of an atom. When an electromotive force is applied through an energy source such as a battery or an outlet, the electrons will jump from nucleus to nucleus along the path of the force.

The rate at which electrons move is called *current*. Current is affected by resistance, which is related to the physical properties of the material through which electrons are moving. In materials with low resistance, like copper wire, electrons are easily persuaded to leave their original nucleus and travel to the next nucleus. Copper wire is a good conductor because electrons are easily conducted, or moved, along the path of the applied electromotive force. High resistance materials, such as rubber, make it nearly impossible for electrons to move from nucleus to nucleus. Rubber does not conduct electrons along the path of applied force. Because it does not allow conduction, rubber is called an *insulator*.

Another type of electricity is static electricity. With static electricity, the electrical particles are not moving; instead a charge has built up in something, like your body after rubbing your feet on carpet. When you rub your feet on the carpet, electrons are transferred from one object to the other. One object, either your feet or the carpet, ends up with extra electrons and a negative charge while the other object is positively charged because it has more protons. For the purposes of this example, let's say your feet are negatively charged and the carpet is positively charged. Then, you touch a neutral object, such as a doorknob, and experience a shock. The shock is actually a tiny lightning bolt that occurs when the extra negatively charged electrons are transferred to the neutrally charged doorknob. The electrons in your body are attracted to the protons in the doorknob and "jump" toward them. At the same time, the electrons already in the doorknob move as far away from the new electrons as possible. In the case of electricity, opposites attract.

Ancient Greeks were familiar with static electricity. They discovered the shocking characteristics of jumping electrons when they rubbed objects on fur. However, moving electricity produced by the application of an electro-

motive force was not discovered until much later. Many people believe Benjamin Franklin discovered electricity. Although this point is debatable, it can be said without doubt that Benjamin Franklin discovered that lightning is a form of electricity through his famous kite-flying experiment. In this experiment, Franklin tied a key to the end of a wet kite string. Then, he flew the kite during a lightning storm. When the lightning struck the key, he felt a spark on his finger and he knew that lightning was a form of electricity.

Thomas Edison is known as the inventor who was first able to capture electricity to produce light. He invented the light bulb and first demonstrated this invention on December 31, 1879 in Menlo Park, NJ. During this demonstration, he said, "We will make electricity so cheap that only the rich will burn candles."

Today, electricity is everywhere. There are lights in our houses, our schools, along our streets, and in our cars. Electricity even runs through our computers, our car engines, our televisions, our radios, and our video games.

IT'S ELECTRIC!

Generalizations

B3   Based on your list and your classifications, write at least three generalizations about the use of electricity.

_____

_____

_____

_____

Classifications

B2   Look at your list of examples. Classify each example into categories. You may not have a "miscellaneous" or "other" category.

_____

_____

_____

_____

Details

B1   List as many examples of the use of electricity as you can in 2 minutes. (You should have at least 25 examples.)

_____

_____

_____

_____

_____

_____

_____

_____

_____

_____

Creative Synthesis

D3 Invent a new way to use electricity. Create an advertisement to sell your new invention to an audience of your choice (your classmates, your teachers, your parents, your city, or another audience). You may use illustrations.

Summarizing

D2 In five sentences or fewer, summarize what happens when you rub your feet on the carpet and then touch a doorknob.

Paraphrasing

D1 In your own words, restate what Thomas Edison meant when he said, "We will make electricity so cheap that only the rich will burn candles."

The Metric System vs. the U.S. Customary System

The metric system and the U.S. customary system are both systems of measurement. So, what is the difference between them and why are there two different systems? In today's global society, wouldn't it be easier if the whole world used the same system?

Elements of the metric system date back to the reign of Louis XVI in France during the 18th century. In 1791, after the French Revolution, the metric system was adopted by the French as the official system of measurement. The goals of the new metric system were to develop a single unit for physical quantity and to create a measurement system that did not require the use of conversion factors. Specifically, all measurements of length are in meters, measurements of liquid are in liters, and measurements of weight are in grams. All three types of measurement use a common set of prefixes that are related to each other by powers of 10. For example, a decameter is 10 meters, a hectometer is 100 meters, and a kilometer is 1,000 meters. Conversely, a decimeter is 1/10 of a meter, a centimeter is 1/100 of a meter, and millimeter is 1/1000 of a meter. There are no conversion factors required to switch among these different representations of the measurement of length. Time is the only unit of measurement that is not unified by the metric system. Time still requires conversion factors to switch among days, hours, minutes, and seconds.

The U.S. customary system can be traced back to the Roman system of measurement. It is based on the Imperial System, which was used by Great Britain until 1995. Today, the United States is the only country that has not converted to the metric system from the customary system, even though the Omnibus Trade and Competitiveness Act of 1988 stated that the metric system is the preferred system for industry and trade. In the United States, the metric system is most commonly used by the military, medical field, and scientific realms. The customary system is used in most other instances. The customary system measures length in inches, feet, yards, and miles; measures general volume in cubic inches, cubic feet, and cubic yards; measures liquid volume in fluid ounces, cups, pints, quarts, and gallons; and measures weight in ounces, pounds, and tons. The customary system requires conversion factors to convert

Customary System			Metric System		
From	Multiply by	To get	From	Multiply by	To get
feet	12	inches	kilometers	1000	meters
pounds	16	ounces	grams	1000	milligrams
quarts	4	cups	liters	10	deciliters

Figure 1. Converting units in the customary system vs. the metric system.

units. For example, to convert feet into yards, you must know that there are 3 feet in one yard. You then would divide the total number of feet by three to determine the total number of yards. Similarly, to convert cups into quarts, you have to know that there are 4 cups in a quart.

The chart in Figure 1 shows the conversion factors needed for the customary system compared to conversion of measurement units within the metric system.

Which system do you think is easier?

THE METRIC SYSTEM VS.
THE U.S. CUSTOMARY SYSTEM

Consequences and Implications

A3 What are the implications of the United States being the only country that has not officially converted to the metric system? Justify your answer.

_____

_____

_____

_____

_____

Cause and Effect

A2 What caused the French to adopt the metric system after the French Revolution? Support your answer.

_____

_____

_____

_____

_____

Sequencing

A1 List the elements of the metric system and the U.S. customary system in the order in which they were discussed in the text.

_____

_____

_____

_____

_____

_____

_____

Main Idea, Theme, or Concept

C3 Theme: Does the overall theme of the text support the use of the U.S. customary system? Why or why not?

_____

_____

_____

_____

_____

Inference

C2 What inferences can be made from the chart in Figure 1? Support your answer with details from the text.

_____

_____

_____

_____

_____

Literary Elements

C1 Imagine a conversation between an American and a French person about the use of the metric system vs. the customary system. Choose one character from this scenario. Describe your chosen character's point of view on this topic. Use details to support your description.

_____

_____

_____

_____

_____

_____

_____

_____

PGIL2025USA

Jacob's Ladder
Reading Comprehension Program

Second Edition

Grade 4

Student Workbook Nonfiction

Contributing Editors:
Joyce VanTassel-Baska,
Tamra Stambaugh,
Kimberley L. Chandler

Contributing Authors:
Heather French,
Paula Ginsburgh,
Tamra Stambaugh,
Joyce VanTassel-Baska

William & Mary
School of Education
CENTER FOR GIFTED EDUCATION

William & Mary
School of Education
Center for Gifted Education
P.O. Box 8795
Williamsburg, VA 23187

First published in 2017 by Prufrock Press Inc.

Published 2021 by Routledge
605 Third Avenue, New York, NY 10017
2 Park Square, Milton Park, Abingdon, Oxon OX14 4RN

Routledge is an imprint of the Taylor & Francis Group, an informa business

Edited by Lacy Compton

Cover and layout design by Raquel Trevino

ISBN-13: 978-1-61821-735-6

NEW YORK AND LONDON

Table of Contents

The American Revolutionary War

In 1765, Americans still considered themselves loyal subjects to the British crown. Great Britain had just finished the Seven Years War with France, during which the Americans helped the British defeat the French on American soil. After the war ended, Great Britain was looking for a way to help pay for the war. Because part of the reason they went to war with France was to protect their colonies in America, the British government decided to pay for the war through taxing Americans. The taxes implemented by the British government were not necessarily high. However, Americans were upset that they were not consulted about the new taxes. The Americans felt it was illegal, or at the very least not fair, to tax them without giving them proper representation within the British parliament. The statement "No taxation without representation" became a well-known phrase during the American Revolutionary War.

The first direct tax against the colonies was the Stamp Act in 1765. The Stamp Act declared that all official documents, newspapers, almanacs, pamphlets, and even playing cards must have official stamps on them. If they did not have stamps, which Americans must buy from Britain, then fines would be charged. Later acts further restricted the activities of Americans. The Currency Act prohibited Americans from printing their own paper money, which hindered trade among the colonies. The Quartering Act mandated that American colonists house British soldiers in their homes, which invaded the colonists' privacy. Colonists began voicing their protests against these taxes and acts. In 1770, the Boston Massacre occurred in Massachusetts. In protest of the Stamp Act and the Tea Act, colonists dumped tea bricks from British ships into Boston Harbor, in what is now known as the Boston Tea Party. During this protest, five Americans were killed.

Because of incidents like this one, as well as philosophical differences between England and the colonies, and America's desire for independence, the American Revolutionary War, also known as the American War of Independence, began in 1775.

In 1776, representatives from each of the 13 colonies met in Philadelphia where they unanimously signed the Declaration of Independence, thereby forming the United States of America. In 1778, the colonists formed an alliance with France. The French helped by sending money, munitions, and troops. These contributions from France helped level the playing field in

the war against Britain. However, the Americans were fighting against a monarchy for the right to establish a democracy. Even though France was helping them win their independence, Americans did not view France as a role model.

During the war, only 1/3 of the colonists, known as Patriots, supported war with Britain, 1/3 of colonists, known as Loyalists, remained loyal to Britain, and 1/3 of colonists remained neutral. However, throughout the war, the Patriots maintained control over 80%–90% of the land. The British were able to capture only a few coastal cities, which they gained through their strong Navy presence.

At the Battle at Saratoga in 1777, one of Britain's main armies was captured, the beginning of the end for the British. In 1781, the British army surrendered at the Battle of Yorktown. This surrender led to the signing of the Treaty of Paris for peace in 1783.

THE AMERICAN REVOLUTIONARY WAR

Main Idea, Theme, or Concept

C3   Concept: What concept represents why the American Revolutionary War was fought? State your answer in five words or less.

_____

_____

_____

Inference

C2   What inferences can be made about the French becoming allies with the Americans during the American Revolutionary War? Justify your answer.

_____

_____

_____

_____

Literary Elements

C1   Choose to be a Patriot, a Loyalist, or a neutral colonist. Describe your character's point of view regarding the war. Support your answer with details.

_____

_____

_____

_____

_____

_____

_____

Creative Synthesis

D3 Write a letter to your family about the American Revolutionary War from the point of view of a colonist, a British soldier, or a French soldier. Be sure to include enough details for the recipient of your letter to understand the war from your point of view.

_____

_____

_____

_____

_____

_____

_____

_____

_____

Summarizing

D2 In three sentences or fewer, summarize the cause(s) of the American Revolutionary War.

_____

_____

_____

_____

_____

Paraphrasing

D1 In your own words, rewrite the following statements:

"No taxation without representation."

_____

_____

"Even though France was helping them win their independence, Americans did not view France as a role model."

_____

_____

The Exploration of Space

The exploration of space gives scientists the opportunity to learn about the sun, stars, and planets. Some space exploration involves scientists called *astronauts* traveling into space. Astronauts use spacecraft, such as space shuttles, to travel beyond the Earth's atmosphere into outer space, which begins about 60 miles above sea level. While in outer space, astronauts explore their surroundings with various tools, such as safety tethering systems to keep their spacesuits attached to the spacecraft (and smaller tethers to attach their tools to their spacesuits). Astronauts might also wear a SAFER or Simplified Aid for EVA Rescue (EVA stands for extravehicular activity, another term for spacewalk). A SAFER is like a backpack that uses small jet thrusters to allow an astronaut to move in space. Other space exploration does not require astronauts but instead uses spacecraft with robots or other mechanical devices, such as satellites, to gather information.

In order for spacecraft, manned or unmanned, to travel into outer space, they must first overcome the pull of Earth's gravity. The heavier an object, the more power is required to break the Earth's gravitational pull. As you can imagine, it takes a tremendous amount of power to launch a space shuttle. These large spacecraft require booster rockets full of fuel to launch them. The boosters burn the fuel that gives off gas bursts that push the spacecraft into the air. The spacecraft eventually reaches a height where the Earth's gravitational pull no longer affects it. Once it passes this point, the shuttle only needs to fire rockets to increase its speed or to change directions.

When a spacecraft is ready to return to Earth, it must first slow down. Once it reenters the atmosphere, it slows down considerably and begins falling toward Earth. The spacecraft deploys, or puts into action, parachutes that further slow down its descent. Spacecraft like space shuttles land on runways just like airplanes. Some of the earlier U.S. spacecraft "splashed down" in the ocean where the astronauts were picked up by boats.

On October 4, 1957, the Soviet Union launched Sputnik, a satellite that orbited Earth, and space exploration officially began. Years later, on April 12, 1961, Yuri A. Gagarin, a Soviet cosmonaut, became the first person to travel to space. In December 1968, the U.S. took the first trip to the moon in

the spacecraft Apollo 8, orbiting the moon 10 times before returning to Earth. Less than a year later, the American astronaut Neil Armstrong became the first person to walk on the moon on July 20, 1969. As Armstrong placed the American flag on the moon, he said, "That's one small step for a man, one giant leap for mankind."

Since this historic landing on the moon, astronauts have continued to explore space by traveling there and by studying the data collected by satellites and other unmanned spacecraft. Through space exploration, astronauts and scientists have learned and continue to learn much about the universe beyond Earth.

THE EXPLORATION OF SPACE

Consequences and Implications

A3   What are the implications of space exploration? Support your answer.

_____

_____

_____

_____

_____

Cause and Effect

A2   What is the effect of the Earth's gravitational pull on spacecraft during launch? During reentry? Support your answer with evidence from the text.

_____

_____

_____

_____

_____

Sequencing

A1   In the space below, create a timeline of the history of space exploration as presented in the text.

Creative Synthesis

D3 Imagine you are an astronaut on the Apollo 8 spacecraft. Write a letter home describing the experience. Be sure to include plenty of details so the recipient of your letter feels like he or she was there with you.

_____

_____

_____

_____

_____

_____

_____

Summarizing

D2 In three sentences or fewer, describe the different ways scientists and astronauts explore space.

_____

_____

_____

_____

_____

Paraphrasing

D1 In your own words, explain what Neil Armstrong meant when he said, "That's one small step for a man, one giant leap for mankind."

_____

_____

_____

_____

_____

_____

_____

Graphic Ice Cream

Tim and Lauren, the owners of Crema, an ice cream shop in Raleigh, NC, surveyed their customers about their favorite ice cream flavors, gathered information about the number of customers on each day of the week, and asked their employees to keep track of how they spend their work hours. They then used different kinds of graphs to represent these data.

Over the period of one month, the Crema owners asked their customers to choose their favorite flavors from a list including chocolate, vanilla, strawberry, banana toffee, strawberry cheesecake, blueberry almond, chocolate raspberry, coffee almond, peach pecan, and caramel pecan. The results are presented in Table 1.

Table 1
Customers' Favorite Flavors

Ice Cream Flavor	Number of Customers' Favorite Flavor
Chocolate	120
Vanilla	65
Strawberry	85
Banana Toffee	190
Strawberry Cheesecake	275
Blueberry Almond	135
Chocolate Raspberry	200
Coffee Almond	95
Peach Pecan	150
Caramel Pecan	75

Tim and Lauren then decided to graph the data they had gathered from their customers. They chose to graph the favorite flavors on a bar graph. A bar graph shows the relationships between groups. On a bar graph, one bar is not affected by another. Bar graphs are a good way to show large differences in results from surveys. They also are excellent tools for determining trends. By using a bar graph to represent the data about customers' favorite flavors, Lauren and Tim will be better able to plan their purchases of ingredients. They will know which ingredients will be used more quickly based on the flavor preferences. The bar graph of Crema customers' favorite flavors is presented in Figure 1.

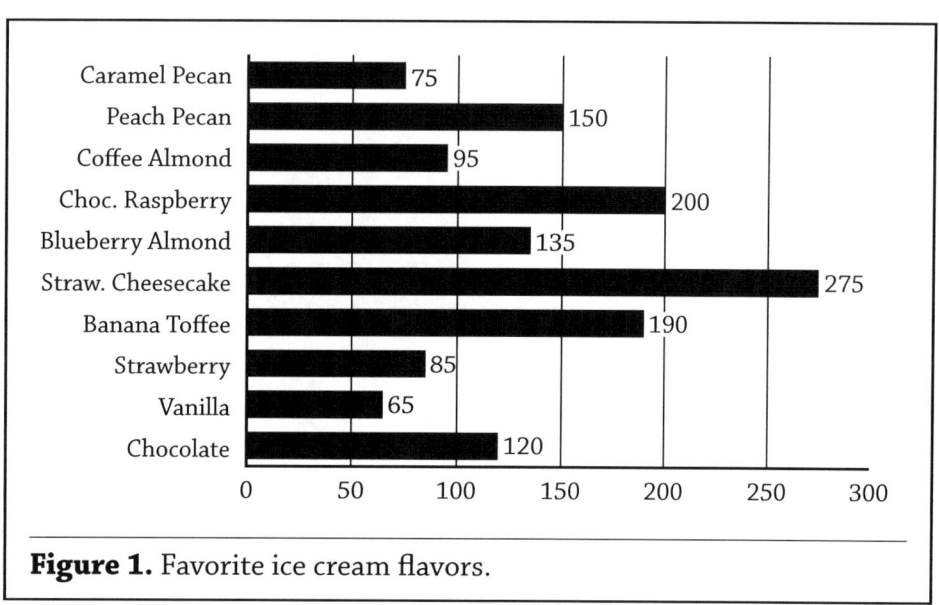

Figure 1. Favorite ice cream flavors.

After realizing how data can help them run their business more efficiently, Tim and Lauren decided to keep track of the number of customers coming to Crema on each day of the week. They were especially interested in Saturday and Sunday. They often wondered if they made or lost money by being open on the weekend. The results of their tracking are presented in Table 2.

Table 2

Number of Customers by Day

Day of the Week	Number of Customers
Monday	95
Tuesday	105
Wednesday	165
Thursday	210
Friday	275
Saturday	150
Sunday	45

Because the bar graph was helpful with comparing favorite flavors, the Crema owners decided to graph these data about customer attendance, too. However, instead of a bar graph, they chose to use a line graph. Line graphs track continuing data where one point is affected by another. With line graphs, there are points on a graph with x- and y-axis coordinates. Points are then joined by a line. Line graphs often are used to track rainfall, the average daily temperature, or, in the case of Crema, the daily number of customers. The line graph they used is presented in Figure 2.

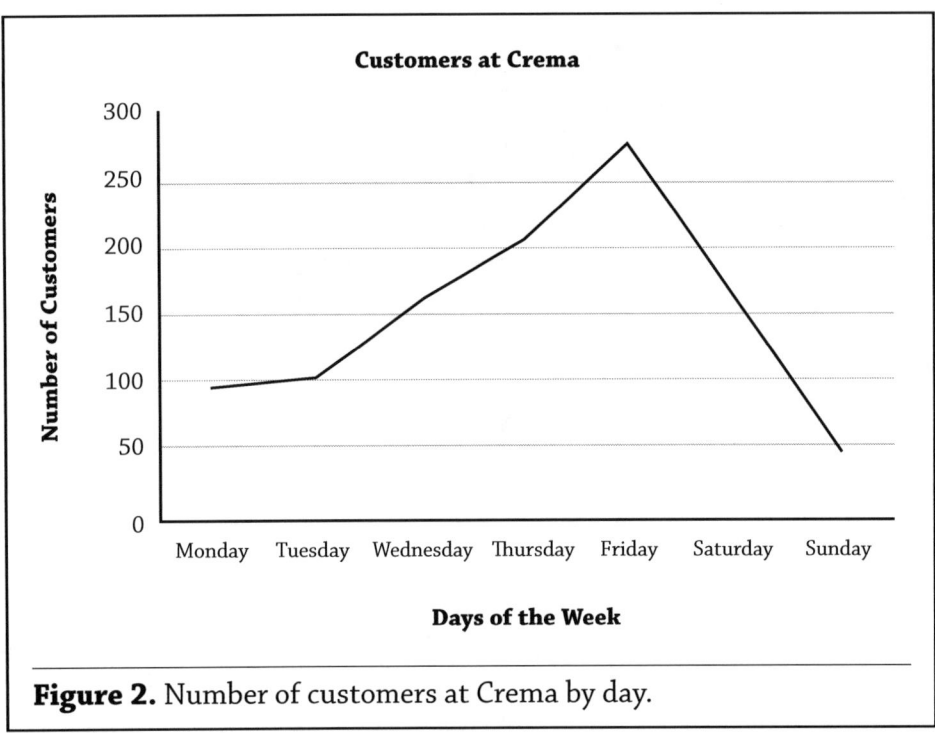

Figure 2. Number of customers at Crema by day.

Tim and Lauren analyzed the data to determine on what days they were most profitable. As they were thinking about money, they wondered how productive their employees were. They decided to ask their employees to keep track of how they spent their work hours. The results of this tracking are presented in Table 3.

Table 3

How Crema Employees Spend a Total Work Day (12 Hours)

Chore	Hours	Percentage of Work Day
Preparing Store to Open	1	8%
Taking Orders	3.5	30%
Preparing Orders	5	42%
Completing Transactions	1	8%
Reconciling Register	.5	4%
Closing	1	8%

The owners of Crema decided to use a circle, or pie, graph to display the data gathered from their employees. Pie graphs are particularly helpful when looking at how a part relates to a whole. In this case, Tim and Lauren wanted to see how the time spent on each chore related to the work day as a whole. The pie chart is presented in Figure 3.

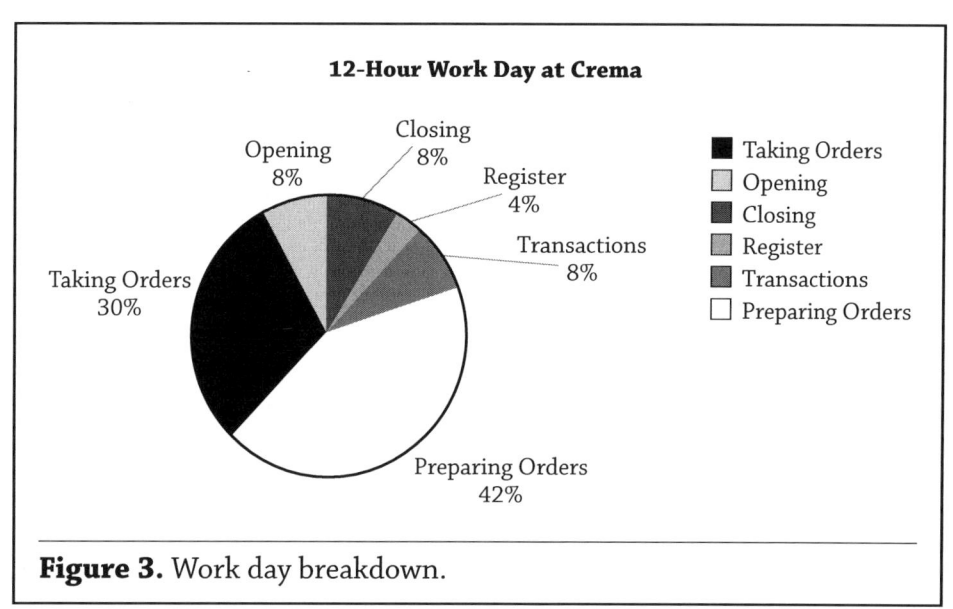

Figure 3. Work day breakdown.

GRAPHIC ICE CREAM

Generalizations

B3 Write at least three generalizations about using graphs to represent data.

_____

_____

_____

_____

Classifications

B2 Look at your list of details. Classify your list into the categories of bar, line, or pie graphs based on which type of graph would be most appropriate for each type of data. Use the definitions from the text to make your classification decisions.

_____

_____

_____

_____

_____

Details

B1 List 15–20 different kinds of data that are often gathered or that could be gathered.

_____

_____

_____

_____

_____

_____

_____

_____

_____

Main Idea, Theme, or Concept

C3 Main Idea: Why did the author title this selection "Graphic Ice Cream"? Use evidence from the text to support your answer.

_____

_____

_____

_____

_____

Inference

C2 What inferences can you draw based on:
- the data and graph about customers' favorite flavors?
- the data and graph about daily customer counts?
- the data and graph about the use of employees' work hours?

_____

_____

_____

_____

_____

_____

Literary Elements

C1 How would you characterize the owners of Crema? Using details from the text to support your answer, describe the kind of business owners they are.

_____

_____

_____

_____

_____

_____

_____

The Great Depression

The Great Depression began in the United States with the stock market crash of 1929. The Depression quickly spread throughout Europe and then the rest of the world.

Economists are divided over what caused the Great Depression. Some believe that at the end of the post-World War I building boom, consumer goods were flooding the market. The supply of goods was far exceeding demand, which caused the economic system to collapse. Others believe that it was a simple case of too many banks playing the stock market with depositors' money. A third theory contends that the Depression deepened because so many people were carrying debt before the crash, and when the crash occurred they simply stopped spending money, which crippled the capitalist market. Another theory blames the severity of the Depression on the extreme drought that struck the Midwest agricultural business during the summer of 1930. Finally, a fifth theory states that it was the collapse of foreign banks that took with it a large amount of U.S. wealth and destroyed the prospect of world trade that caused the Depression to become a Great Depression.

Regardless of the cause, the Great Depression was one of the saddest periods in U.S. history. During this time period from 1929 to 1941, Americans endured much hardship. In the Midwest, farmers experienced an intense drought that earned this agricultural area the name "Dust Bowl." During the summer of 1930, many Midwest farmers were forced to leave their lands because of dust storms that blew much of the soil away. The dust storms were caused by a failure to rotate crops and the exposure of soil by the removal of grass through plowing. With the drought, the soil dried out, became dust, and then blew away in black clouds. Much of the soil was lost in the Atlantic Ocean as it blew eastward. Many people in the Midwest suffered from dust pneumonia and malnutrition.

In other areas of the country, conditions were not any better. Unemployment rose from 5 million people without jobs in 1930 to 11 million people without jobs in 1931. A staggering 25% of Americans were unemployed. Many people lost their homes. Sadly, 20% of children were hungry and did not have proper clothing or houses. Many schools closed because they could not afford to stay open. Of young people between the ages of 16 and 24, 40% of them were neither in school nor working. Children wrote letters to the First Lady, Eleanor Roosevelt, begging her to help them find food, clothing, and shelter.

After his inauguration in 1933, President Franklin D. Roosevelt passed the New Deal legislation. The New Deal restructured the economy and increased government spending to stimulate demand within the market, create jobs, and provide relief for the poor and unemployed. However, in 1937, the American economy took another nosedive that further deepened the Great Depression. During the period of the Depression, most countries experienced political upheaval that allowed dictators like Hitler, Stalin, and Mussolini to rise to power, leading to the beginning of World War II in 1939.

Supplying materials and resources for troops to protect the world against Nazi Germany stimulated economies in Europe from 1937–1939, pulling these nations out of depression. In the U.S., jobs increased, people worked overtime to make up for lost wages, and Americans agreed to rations for the first time in support of the war effort. The President pushed for a large quantity of war supplies no matter what it cost the government. In the United States, the Great Depression ended in 1941 when America entered World War II.

THE GREAT DEPRESSION

Consequences and Implications

A3   What were the consequences of the Great Depression for children? Justify your answer with supporting details.

_____

_____

_____

Cause and Effect

A2   What caused the end of the Great Depression in Europe? In America? Support your answer.

_____

_____

_____

_____

_____

_____

Sequencing

A1   List, in order, the events of the Great Depression as discussed in the text.

_____

_____

_____

_____

_____

_____

_____

_____

_____

Generalizations

B3   Write at least three generalizations about your life today compared to the life of a child during the Great Depression.

_____

_____

_____

_____

Classifications

B2   Study your list. Classify your details into categories. You may not have a "miscellaneous" or "other" category.

_____

_____

_____

_____

_____

_____

_____

Details

B1   List at least 25 things and/or privileges that you have today that you would not have had growing up during the Great Depression.

_____

_____

_____

_____

_____

_____

_____

_____

_____

It's Electric!

How much do you know about electricity? Electricity refers to the movement of charged particles within atoms. There are two kinds of charged particles: Electrons have a negative charge, and protons have a positive charge. Electrons are constantly orbiting the nucleus of an atom. When an electromotive force is applied through an energy source such as a battery or an outlet, the electrons will jump from nucleus to nucleus along the path of the force.

The rate at which electrons move is called *current*. Current is affected by resistance, which is related to the physical properties of the material through which electrons are moving. In materials with low resistance, like copper wire, electrons are easily persuaded to leave their original nucleus and travel to the next nucleus. Copper wire is a good conductor because electrons are easily conducted, or moved, along the path of the applied electromotive force. High resistance materials, such as rubber, make it nearly impossible for electrons to move from nucleus to nucleus. Rubber does not conduct electrons along the path of applied force. Because it does not allow conduction, rubber is called an *insulator*.

Another type of electricity is static electricity. With static electricity, the electrical particles are not moving; instead a charge has built up in something, like your body after rubbing your feet on carpet. When you rub your feet on the carpet, electrons are transferred from one object to the other. One object, either your feet or the carpet, ends up with extra electrons and a negative charge while the other object is positively charged because it has more protons. For the purposes of this example, let's say your feet are negatively charged and the carpet is positively charged. Then, you touch a neutral object, such as a doorknob, and experience a shock. The shock is actually a tiny lightning bolt that occurs when the extra negatively charged electrons are transferred to the neutrally charged doorknob. The electrons in your body are attracted to the protons in the doorknob and "jump" toward them. At the same time, the electrons already in the doorknob move as far away from the new electrons as possible. In the case of electricity, opposites attract.

Ancient Greeks were familiar with static electricity. They discovered the shocking characteristics of jumping electrons when they rubbed objects on fur. However, moving electricity produced by the application of an electro-

motive force was not discovered until much later. Many people believe Benjamin Franklin discovered electricity. Although this point is debatable, it can be said without doubt that Benjamin Franklin discovered that lightning is a form of electricity through his famous kite-flying experiment. In this experiment, Franklin tied a key to the end of a wet kite string. Then, he flew the kite during a lightning storm. When the lightning struck the key, he felt a spark on his finger and he knew that lightning was a form of electricity.

Thomas Edison is known as the inventor who was first able to capture electricity to produce light. He invented the light bulb and first demonstrated this invention on December 31, 1879 in Menlo Park, NJ. During this demonstration, he said, "We will make electricity so cheap that only the rich will burn candles."

Today, electricity is everywhere. There are lights in our houses, our schools, along our streets, and in our cars. Electricity even runs through our computers, our car engines, our televisions, our radios, and our video games.

IT'S ELECTRIC!

Generalizations

B3 Based on your list and your classifications, write at least three generalizations about the use of electricity.

_____

_____

_____

_____

Classifications

B2 Look at your list of examples. Classify each example into categories. You may not have a "miscellaneous" or "other" category.

_____

_____

_____

_____

Details

B1 List as many examples of the use of electricity as you can in 2 minutes. (You should have at least 25 examples.)

_____

_____

_____

_____

_____

_____

_____

_____

Creative Synthesis

D3 Invent a new way to use electricity. Create an advertisement to sell your new invention to an audience of your choice (your classmates, your teachers, your parents, your city, or another audience). You may use illustrations.

Summarizing

D2 In five sentences or fewer, summarize what happens when you rub your feet on the carpet and then touch a doorknob.

_____

_____

_____

_____

_____

_____

Paraphrasing

D1 In your own words, restate what Thomas Edison meant when he said, "We will make electricity so cheap that only the rich will burn candles."

_____

_____

_____

_____

_____

The Metric System vs. the U.S. Customary System

The metric system and the U.S. customary system are both systems of measurement. So, what is the difference between them and why are there two different systems? In today's global society, wouldn't it be easier if the whole world used the same system?

Elements of the metric system date back to the reign of Louis XVI in France during the 18th century. In 1791, after the French Revolution, the metric system was adopted by the French as the official system of measurement. The goals of the new metric system were to develop a single unit for physical quantity and to create a measurement system that did not require the use of conversion factors. Specifically, all measurements of length are in meters, measurements of liquid are in liters, and measurements of weight are in grams. All three types of measurement use a common set of prefixes that are related to each other by powers of 10. For example, a decameter is 10 meters, a hectometer is 100 meters, and a kilometer is 1,000 meters. Conversely, a decimeter is 1/10 of a meter, a centimeter is 1/100 of a meter, and millimeter is 1/1000 of a meter. There are no conversion factors required to switch among these different representations of the measurement of length. Time is the only unit of measurement that is not unified by the metric system. Time still requires conversion factors to switch among days, hours, minutes, and seconds.

The U.S. customary system can be traced back to the Roman system of measurement. It is based on the Imperial System, which was used by Great Britain until 1995. Today, the United States is the only country that has not converted to the metric system from the customary system, even though the Omnibus Trade and Competitiveness Act of 1988 stated that the metric system is the preferred system for industry and trade. In the United States, the metric system is most commonly used by the military, medical field, and scientific realms. The customary system is used in most other instances. The customary system measures length in inches, feet, yards, and miles; measures general volume in cubic inches, cubic feet, and cubic yards; measures liquid volume in fluid ounces, cups, pints, quarts, and gallons; and measures weight in ounces, pounds, and tons. The customary system requires conversion factors to convert

Customary System			Metric System		
From	Multiply by	To get	From	Multiply by	To get
feet	12	inches	kilometers	1000	meters
pounds	16	ounces	grams	1000	milligrams
quarts	4	cups	liters	10	deciliters

Figure 1. Converting units in the customary system vs. the metric system.

units. For example, to convert feet into yards, you must know that there are 3 feet in one yard. You then would divide the total number of feet by three to determine the total number of yards. Similarly, to convert cups into quarts, you have to know that there are 4 cups in a quart.

The chart in Figure 1 shows the conversion factors needed for the customary system compared to conversion of measurement units within the metric system.

Which system do you think is easier?

THE METRIC SYSTEM VS. THE U.S. CUSTOMARY SYSTEM

Consequences and Implications

A3   What are the implications of the United States being the only country that has not officially converted to the metric system? Justify your answer.

_____

_____

_____

_____

_____

Cause and Effect

A2   What caused the French to adopt the metric system after the French Revolution? Support your answer.

_____

_____

_____

_____

_____

Sequencing

A1   List the elements of the metric system and the U.S. customary system in the order in which they were discussed in the text.

_____

_____

_____

_____

_____

_____

Main Idea, Theme, or Concept

C3   Theme: Does the overall theme of the text support the use of the U.S. customary system? Why or why not?

_____

_____

_____

_____

_____

Inference

C2   What inferences can be made from the chart in Figure 1? Support your answer with details from the text.

_____

_____

_____

_____

_____

Literary Elements

C1   Imagine a conversation between an American and a French person about the use of the metric system vs. the customary system. Choose one character from this scenario. Describe your chosen character's point of view on this topic. Use details to support your description.

_____

_____

_____

_____

_____

_____

_____

_____

PGIL2025USA

Jacob's Ladder

Reading Comprehension Program

Second Edition

Grade

4

Student Workbook Nonfiction

Contributing Editors:
Joyce VanTassel-Baska,
Tamra Stambaugh,
Kimberley L. Chandler

Contributing Authors:
Heather French,
Paula Ginsburgh,
Tamra Stambaugh,
Joyce VanTassel-Baska

William & Mary
School of Education

CENTER FOR GIFTED EDUCATION

William & Mary
School of Education
Center for Gifted Education
P.O. Box 8795
Williamsburg, VA 23187

First published in 2017 by Prufrock Press Inc.

Published 2021 by Routledge
605 Third Avenue, New York, NY 10017
2 Park Square, Milton Park, Abingdon, Oxon OX14 4RN

Routledge is an imprint of the Taylor & Francis Group, an informa business

Edited by Lacy Compton

Cover and layout design by Raquel Trevino

ISBN-13: 978-1-61821-735-6

NEW YORK AND LONDON

Table of Contents

The American Revolutionary War

In 1765, Americans still considered themselves loyal subjects to the British crown. Great Britain had just finished the Seven Years War with France, during which the Americans helped the British defeat the French on American soil. After the war ended, Great Britain was looking for a way to help pay for the war. Because part of the reason they went to war with France was to protect their colonies in America, the British government decided to pay for the war through taxing Americans. The taxes implemented by the British government were not necessarily high. However, Americans were upset that they were not consulted about the new taxes. The Americans felt it was illegal, or at the very least not fair, to tax them without giving them proper representation within the British parliament. The statement "No taxation without representation" became a well-known phrase during the American Revolutionary War.

The first direct tax against the colonies was the Stamp Act in 1765. The Stamp Act declared that all official documents, newspapers, almanacs, pamphlets, and even playing cards must have official stamps on them. If they did not have stamps, which Americans must buy from Britain, then fines would be charged. Later acts further restricted the activities of Americans. The Currency Act prohibited Americans from printing their own paper money, which hindered trade among the colonies. The Quartering Act mandated that American colonists house British soldiers in their homes, which invaded the colonists' privacy. Colonists began voicing their protests against these taxes and acts. In 1770, the Boston Massacre occurred in Massachusetts. In protest of the Stamp Act and the Tea Act, colonists dumped tea bricks from British ships into Boston Harbor, in what is now known as the Boston Tea Party. During this protest, five Americans were killed.

Because of incidents like this one, as well as philosophical differences between England and the colonies, and America's desire for independence, the American Revolutionary War, also known as the American War of Independence, began in 1775.

In 1776, representatives from each of the 13 colonies met in Philadelphia where they unanimously signed the Declaration of Independence, thereby forming the United States of America. In 1778, the colonists formed an alliance with France. The French helped by sending money, munitions, and troops. These contributions from France helped level the playing field in

the war against Britain. However, the Americans were fighting against a monarchy for the right to establish a democracy. Even though France was helping them win their independence, Americans did not view France as a role model.

During the war, only 1/3 of the colonists, known as Patriots, supported war with Britain, 1/3 of colonists, known as Loyalists, remained loyal to Britain, and 1/3 of colonists remained neutral. However, throughout the war, the Patriots maintained control over 80%–90% of the land. The British were able to capture only a few coastal cities, which they gained through their strong Navy presence.

At the Battle at Saratoga in 1777, one of Britain's main armies was captured, the beginning of the end for the British. In 1781, the British army surrendered at the Battle of Yorktown. This surrender led to the signing of the Treaty of Paris for peace in 1783.

THE AMERICAN REVOLUTIONARY WAR

Main Idea, Theme, or Concept

C3 Concept: What concept represents why the American Revolutionary War was fought? State your answer in five words or less.

_____

_____

_____

Inference

C2 What inferences can be made about the French becoming allies with the Americans during the American Revolutionary War? Justify your answer.

_____

_____

_____

_____

Literary Elements

C1 Choose to be a Patriot, a Loyalist, or a neutral colonist. Describe your character's point of view regarding the war. Support your answer with details.

_____

_____

_____

_____

_____

_____

_____

_____

Creative Synthesis

D3 Write a letter to your family about the American Revolutionary War from the point of view of a colonist, a British soldier, or a French soldier. Be sure to include enough details for the recipient of your letter to understand the war from your point of view.

_____

_____

_____

_____

_____

_____

_____

_____

_____

Summarizing

D2 In three sentences or fewer, summarize the cause(s) of the American Revolutionary War.

_____

_____

_____

_____

_____

Paraphrasing

D1 In your own words, rewrite the following statements:

"No taxation without representation."

_____

"Even though France was helping them win their independence, Americans did not view France as a role model."

_____

_____

The Exploration of Space

The exploration of space gives scientists the opportunity to learn about the sun, stars, and planets. Some space exploration involves scientists called *astronauts* traveling into space. Astronauts use spacecraft, such as space shuttles, to travel beyond the Earth's atmosphere into outer space, which begins about 60 miles above sea level. While in outer space, astronauts explore their surroundings with various tools, such as safety tethering systems to keep their spacesuits attached to the spacecraft (and smaller tethers to attach their tools to their spacesuits). Astronauts might also wear a SAFER or Simplified Aid for EVA Rescue (EVA stands for extravehicular activity, another term for spacewalk). A SAFER is like a backpack that uses small jet thrusters to allow an astronaut to move in space. Other space exploration does not require astronauts but instead uses spacecraft with robots or other mechanical devices, such as satellites, to gather information.

In order for spacecraft, manned or unmanned, to travel into outer space, they must first overcome the pull of Earth's gravity. The heavier an object, the more power is required to break the Earth's gravitational pull. As you can imagine, it takes a tremendous amount of power to launch a space shuttle. These large spacecraft require booster rockets full of fuel to launch them. The boosters burn the fuel that gives off gas bursts that push the spacecraft into the air. The spacecraft eventually reaches a height where the Earth's gravitational pull no longer affects it. Once it passes this point, the shuttle only needs to fire rockets to increase its speed or to change directions.

When a spacecraft is ready to return to Earth, it must first slow down. Once it reenters the atmosphere, it slows down considerably and begins falling toward Earth. The spacecraft deploys, or puts into action, parachutes that further slow down its descent. Spacecraft like space shuttles land on runways just like airplanes. Some of the earlier U.S. spacecraft "splashed down" in the ocean where the astronauts were picked up by boats.

On October 4, 1957, the Soviet Union launched Sputnik, a satellite that orbited Earth, and space exploration officially began. Years later, on April 12, 1961, Yuri A. Gagarin, a Soviet cosmonaut, became the first person to travel to space. In December 1968, the U.S. took the first trip to the moon in

the spacecraft Apollo 8, orbiting the moon 10 times before returning to Earth. Less than a year later, the American astronaut Neil Armstrong became the first person to walk on the moon on July 20, 1969. As Armstrong placed the American flag on the moon, he said, "That's one small step for a man, one giant leap for mankind."

Since this historic landing on the moon, astronauts have continued to explore space by traveling there and by studying the data collected by satellites and other unmanned spacecraft. Through space exploration, astronauts and scientists have learned and continue to learn much about the universe beyond Earth.

THE EXPLORATION OF SPACE

Consequences and Implications

A3 What are the implications of space exploration? Support your answer.

_____

_____

_____

_____

_____

Cause and Effect

A2 What is the effect of the Earth's gravitational pull on spacecraft during launch? During reentry? Support your answer with evidence from the text.

_____

_____

_____

_____

_____

Sequencing

A1 In the space below, create a timeline of the history of space exploration as presented in the text.

Creative Synthesis

D3   Imagine you are an astronaut on the Apollo 8 spacecraft. Write a letter home describing the experience. Be sure to include plenty of details so the recipient of your letter feels like he or she was there with you.

_____

_____

_____

_____

_____

_____

_____

Summarizing

D2   In three sentences or fewer, describe the different ways scientists and astronauts explore space.

_____

_____

_____

_____

_____

_____

Paraphrasing

D1   In your own words, explain what Neil Armstrong meant when he said, "That's one small step for a man, one giant leap for mankind."

_____

_____

_____

_____

_____

_____

Graphic Ice Cream

Tim and Lauren, the owners of Crema, an ice cream shop in Raleigh, NC, surveyed their customers about their favorite ice cream flavors, gathered information about the number of customers on each day of the week, and asked their employees to keep track of how they spend their work hours. They then used different kinds of graphs to represent these data.

Over the period of one month, the Crema owners asked their customers to choose their favorite flavors from a list including chocolate, vanilla, strawberry, banana toffee, strawberry cheesecake, blueberry almond, chocolate raspberry, coffee almond, peach pecan, and caramel pecan. The results are presented in Table 1.

Table 1

Customers' Favorite Flavors

Ice Cream Flavor	Number of Customers' Favorite Flavor
Chocolate	120
Vanilla	65
Strawberry	85
Banana Toffee	190
Strawberry Cheesecake	275
Blueberry Almond	135
Chocolate Raspberry	200
Coffee Almond	95
Peach Pecan	150
Caramel Pecan	75

Tim and Lauren then decided to graph the data they had gathered from their customers. They chose to graph the favorite flavors on a bar graph. A bar graph shows the relationships between groups. On a bar graph, one bar is not affected by another. Bar graphs are a good way to show large differences in results from surveys. They also are excellent tools for determining trends. By using a bar graph to represent the data about customers' favorite flavors, Lauren and Tim will be better able to plan their purchases of ingredients. They will know which ingredients will be used more quickly based on the flavor preferences. The bar graph of Crema customers' favorite flavors is presented in Figure 1.

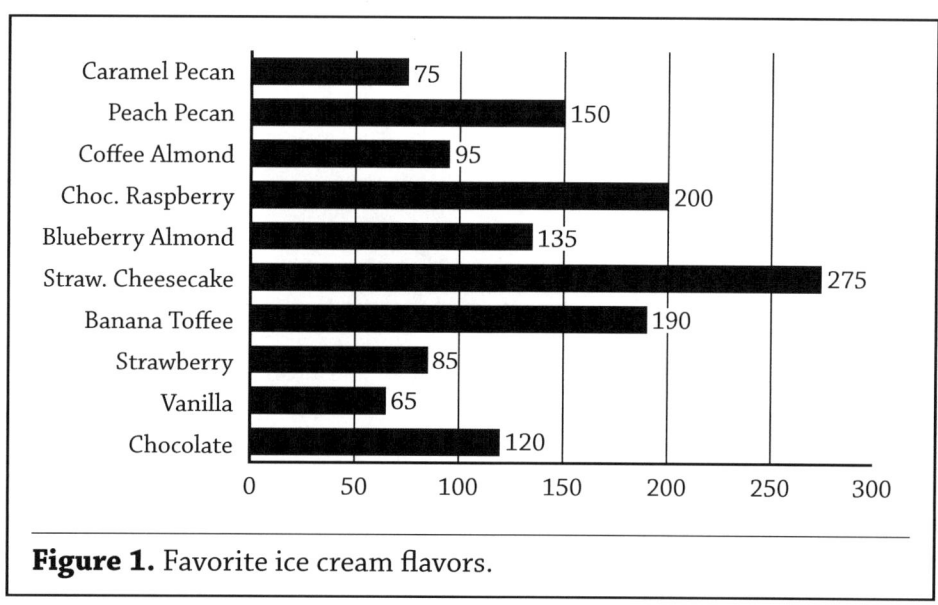

Figure 1. Favorite ice cream flavors.

After realizing how data can help them run their business more efficiently, Tim and Lauren decided to keep track of the number of customers coming to Crema on each day of the week. They were especially interested in Saturday and Sunday. They often wondered if they made or lost money by being open on the weekend. The results of their tracking are presented in Table 2.

Table 2

Number of Customers by Day

Day of the Week	Number of Customers
Monday	95
Tuesday	105
Wednesday	165
Thursday	210
Friday	275
Saturday	150
Sunday	45

Because the bar graph was helpful with comparing favorite flavors, the Crema owners decided to graph these data about customer attendance, too. However, instead of a bar graph, they chose to use a line graph. Line graphs track continuing data where one point is affected by another. With line graphs, there are points on a graph with x- and y-axis coordinates. Points are then joined by a line. Line graphs often are used to track rainfall, the average daily temperature, or, in the case of Crema, the daily number of customers. The line graph they used is presented in Figure 2.

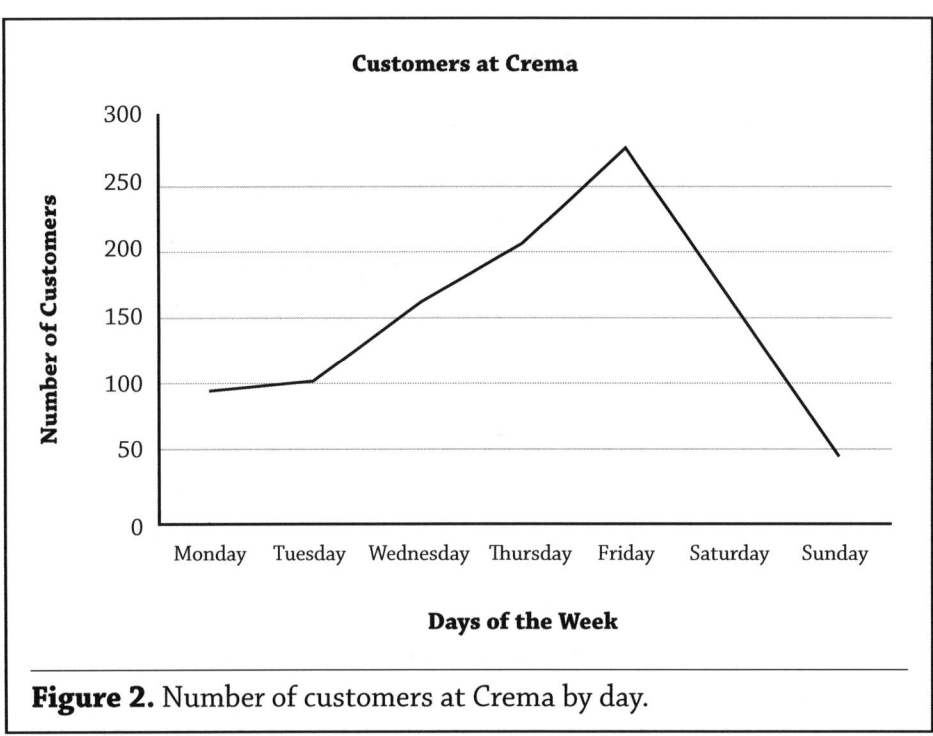

Figure 2. Number of customers at Crema by day.

Tim and Lauren analyzed the data to determine on what days they were most profitable. As they were thinking about money, they wondered how productive their employees were. They decided to ask their employees to keep track of how they spent their work hours. The results of this tracking are presented in Table 3.

Table 3

How Crema Employees Spend a Total Work Day (12 Hours)

Chore	Hours	Percentage of Work Day
Preparing Store to Open	1	8%
Taking Orders	3.5	30%
Preparing Orders	5	42%
Completing Transactions	1	8%
Reconciling Register	.5	4%
Closing	1	8%

The owners of Crema decided to use a circle, or pie, graph to display the data gathered from their employees. Pie graphs are particularly helpful when looking at how a part relates to a whole. In this case, Tim and Lauren wanted to see how the time spent on each chore related to the work day as a whole. The pie chart is presented in Figure 3.

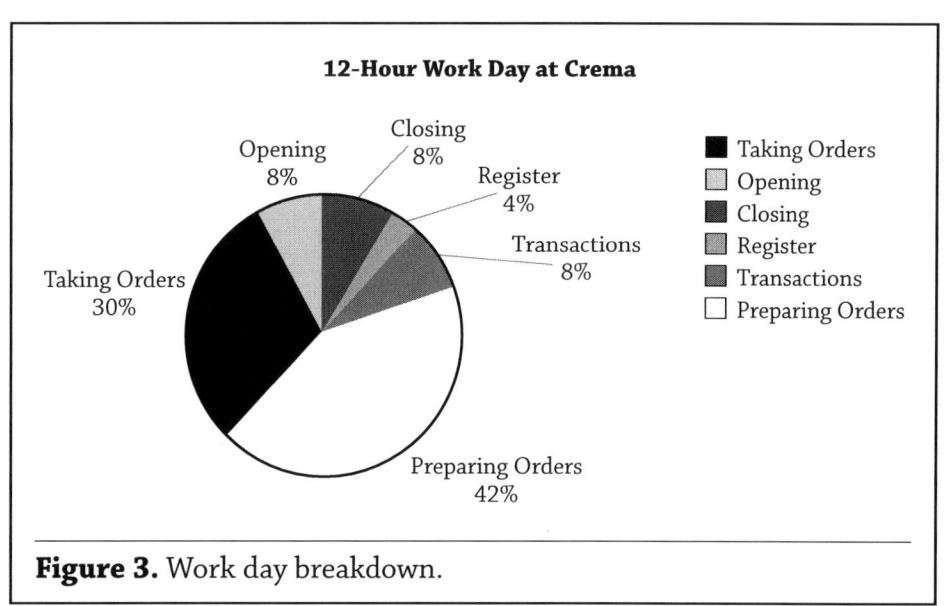

Figure 3. Work day breakdown.

GRAPHIC ICE CREAM

Generalizations

B3 Write at least three generalizations about using graphs to represent data.

_____

_____

_____

_____

Classifications

B2 Look at your list of details. Classify your list into the categories of bar, line, or pie graphs based on which type of graph would be most appropriate for each type of data. Use the definitions from the text to make your classification decisions.

_____

_____

_____

_____

_____

Details

B1 List 15–20 different kinds of data that are often gathered or that could be gathered.

_____

_____

_____

_____

_____

_____

_____

_____

_____

Main Idea, Theme, or Concept

C3   Main Idea: Why did the author title this selection "Graphic Ice Cream"? Use evidence from the text to support your answer.

_____

_____

_____

_____

_____

Inference

C2   What inferences can you draw based on:
- the data and graph about customers' favorite flavors?
- the data and graph about daily customer counts?
- the data and graph about the use of employees' work hours?

_____

_____

_____

_____

_____

_____

Literary Elements

C1   How would you characterize the owners of Crema? Using details from the text to support your answer, describe the kind of business owners they are.

_____

_____

_____

_____

_____

_____

_____

_____

The Great Depression

The Great Depression began in the United States with the stock market crash of 1929. The Depression quickly spread throughout Europe and then the rest of the world.

Economists are divided over what caused the Great Depression. Some believe that at the end of the post-World War I building boom, consumer goods were flooding the market. The supply of goods was far exceeding demand, which caused the economic system to collapse. Others believe that it was a simple case of too many banks playing the stock market with depositors' money. A third theory contends that the Depression deepened because so many people were carrying debt before the crash, and when the crash occurred they simply stopped spending money, which crippled the capitalist market. Another theory blames the severity of the Depression on the extreme drought that struck the Midwest agricultural business during the summer of 1930. Finally, a fifth theory states that it was the collapse of foreign banks that took with it a large amount of U.S. wealth and destroyed the prospect of world trade that caused the Depression to become a Great Depression.

Regardless of the cause, the Great Depression was one of the saddest periods in U.S. history. During this time period from 1929 to 1941, Americans endured much hardship. In the Midwest, farmers experienced an intense drought that earned this agricultural area the name "Dust Bowl." During the summer of 1930, many Midwest farmers were forced to leave their lands because of dust storms that blew much of the soil away. The dust storms were caused by a failure to rotate crops and the exposure of soil by the removal of grass through plowing. With the drought, the soil dried out, became dust, and then blew away in black clouds. Much of the soil was lost in the Atlantic Ocean as it blew eastward. Many people in the Midwest suffered from dust pneumonia and malnutrition.

In other areas of the country, conditions were not any better. Unemployment rose from 5 million people without jobs in 1930 to 11 million people without jobs in 1931. A staggering 25% of Americans were unemployed. Many people lost their homes. Sadly, 20% of children were hungry and did not have proper clothing or houses. Many schools closed because they could not afford to stay open. Of young people between the ages of 16 and 24, 40% of them were neither in school nor working. Children wrote letters to the First Lady, Eleanor Roosevelt, begging her to help them find food, clothing, and shelter.

After his inauguration in 1933, President Franklin D. Roosevelt passed the New Deal legislation. The New Deal restructured the economy and increased government spending to stimulate demand within the market, create jobs, and provide relief for the poor and unemployed. However, in 1937, the American economy took another nosedive that further deepened the Great Depression. During the period of the Depression, most countries experienced political upheaval that allowed dictators like Hitler, Stalin, and Mussolini to rise to power, leading to the beginning of World War II in 1939.

Supplying materials and resources for troops to protect the world against Nazi Germany stimulated economies in Europe from 1937–1939, pulling these nations out of depression. In the U.S., jobs increased, people worked overtime to make up for lost wages, and Americans agreed to rations for the first time in support of the war effort. The President pushed for a large quantity of war supplies no matter what it cost the government. In the United States, the Great Depression ended in 1941 when America entered World War II.

THE GREAT DEPRESSION

Consequences and Implications

A3 What were the consequences of the Great Depression for children? Justify your answer with supporting details.

_____

_____

_____

Cause and Effect

A2 What caused the end of the Great Depression in Europe? In America? Support your answer.

_____

_____

_____

_____

_____

_____

Sequencing

A1 List, in order, the events of the Great Depression as discussed in the text.

_____

_____

_____

_____

_____

_____

_____

_____

_____

Generalizations

B3   Write at least three generalizations about your life today compared to the life of a child during the Great Depression.

_____

_____

_____

_____

Classifications

B2   Study your list. Classify your details into categories. You may not have a "miscellaneous" or "other" category.

_____

_____

_____

_____

_____

_____

_____

_____

Details

B1   List at least 25 things and/or privileges that you have today that you would not have had growing up during the Great Depression.

_____

_____

_____

_____

_____

_____

_____

_____

_____

_____

It's Electric!

How much do you know about electricity? Electricity refers to the movement of charged particles within atoms. There are two kinds of charged particles: Electrons have a negative charge, and protons have a positive charge. Electrons are constantly orbiting the nucleus of an atom. When an electromotive force is applied through an energy source such as a battery or an outlet, the electrons will jump from nucleus to nucleus along the path of the force.

The rate at which electrons move is called *current*. Current is affected by resistance, which is related to the physical properties of the material through which electrons are moving. In materials with low resistance, like copper wire, electrons are easily persuaded to leave their original nucleus and travel to the next nucleus. Copper wire is a good conductor because electrons are easily conducted, or moved, along the path of the applied electromotive force. High resistance materials, such as rubber, make it nearly impossible for electrons to move from nucleus to nucleus. Rubber does not conduct electrons along the path of applied force. Because it does not allow conduction, rubber is called an *insulator*.

Another type of electricity is static electricity. With static electricity, the electrical particles are not moving; instead a charge has built up in something, like your body after rubbing your feet on carpet. When you rub your feet on the carpet, electrons are transferred from one object to the other. One object, either your feet or the carpet, ends up with extra electrons and a negative charge while the other object is positively charged because it has more protons. For the purposes of this example, let's say your feet are negatively charged and the carpet is positively charged. Then, you touch a neutral object, such as a doorknob, and experience a shock. The shock is actually a tiny lightning bolt that occurs when the extra negatively charged electrons are transferred to the neutrally charged doorknob. The electrons in your body are attracted to the protons in the doorknob and "jump" toward them. At the same time, the electrons already in the doorknob move as far away from the new electrons as possible. In the case of electricity, opposites attract.

Ancient Greeks were familiar with static electricity. They discovered the shocking characteristics of jumping electrons when they rubbed objects on fur. However, moving electricity produced by the application of an electro-

motive force was not discovered until much later. Many people believe Benjamin Franklin discovered electricity. Although this point is debatable, it can be said without doubt that Benjamin Franklin discovered that lightning is a form of electricity through his famous kite-flying experiment. In this experiment, Franklin tied a key to the end of a wet kite string. Then, he flew the kite during a lightning storm. When the lightning struck the key, he felt a spark on his finger and he knew that lightning was a form of electricity.

Thomas Edison is known as the inventor who was first able to capture electricity to produce light. He invented the light bulb and first demonstrated this invention on December 31, 1879 in Menlo Park, NJ. During this demonstration, he said, "We will make electricity so cheap that only the rich will burn candles."

Today, electricity is everywhere. There are lights in our houses, our schools, along our streets, and in our cars. Electricity even runs through our computers, our car engines, our televisions, our radios, and our video games.

IT'S ELECTRIC!

Generalizations

B3 Based on your list and your classifications, write at least three generalizations about the use of electricity.

_____

_____

_____

_____

Classifications

B2 Look at your list of examples. Classify each example into categories. You may not have a "miscellaneous" or "other" category.

_____

_____

_____

_____

Details

B1 List as many examples of the use of electricity as you can in 2 minutes. (You should have at least 25 examples.)

_____

_____

_____

_____

_____

_____

_____

_____

_____

Creative Synthesis

D3 Invent a new way to use electricity. Create an advertisement to sell your new invention to an audience of your choice (your classmates, your teachers, your parents, your city, or another audience). You may use illustrations.

Summarizing

D2 In five sentences or fewer, summarize what happens when you rub your feet on the carpet and then touch a doorknob.

_____

_____

_____

_____

_____

_____

Paraphrasing

D1 In your own words, restate what Thomas Edison meant when he said, "We will make electricity so cheap that only the rich will burn candles."

_____

_____

_____

_____

_____

The Metric System vs. the U.S. Customary System

The metric system and the U.S. customary system are both systems of measurement. So, what is the difference between them and why are there two different systems? In today's global society, wouldn't it be easier if the whole world used the same system?

Elements of the metric system date back to the reign of Louis XVI in France during the 18th century. In 1791, after the French Revolution, the metric system was adopted by the French as the official system of measurement. The goals of the new metric system were to develop a single unit for physical quantity and to create a measurement system that did not require the use of conversion factors. Specifically, all measurements of length are in meters, measurements of liquid are in liters, and measurements of weight are in grams. All three types of measurement use a common set of prefixes that are related to each other by powers of 10. For example, a decameter is 10 meters, a hectometer is 100 meters, and a kilometer is 1,000 meters. Conversely, a decimeter is 1/10 of a meter, a centimeter is 1/100 of a meter, and millimeter is 1/1000 of a meter. There are no conversion factors required to switch among these different representations of the measurement of length. Time is the only unit of measurement that is not unified by the metric system. Time still requires conversion factors to switch among days, hours, minutes, and seconds.

The U.S. customary system can be traced back to the Roman system of measurement. It is based on the Imperial System, which was used by Great Britain until 1995. Today, the United States is the only country that has not converted to the metric system from the customary system, even though the Omnibus Trade and Competitiveness Act of 1988 stated that the metric system is the preferred system for industry and trade. In the United States, the metric system is most commonly used by the military, medical field, and scientific realms. The customary system is used in most other instances. The customary system measures length in inches, feet, yards, and miles; measures general volume in cubic inches, cubic feet, and cubic yards; measures liquid volume in fluid ounces, cups, pints, quarts, and gallons; and measures weight in ounces, pounds, and tons. The customary system requires conversion factors to convert

Customary System			Metric System		
From	Multiply by	To get	From	Multiply by	To get
feet	12	inches	kilometers	1000	meters
pounds	16	ounces	grams	1000	milligrams
quarts	4	cups	liters	10	deciliters

Figure 1. Converting units in the customary system vs. the metric system.

units. For example, to convert feet into yards, you must know that there are 3 feet in one yard. You then would divide the total number of feet by three to determine the total number of yards. Similarly, to convert cups into quarts, you have to know that there are 4 cups in a quart.

The chart in Figure 1 shows the conversion factors needed for the customary system compared to conversion of measurement units within the metric system.

Which system do you think is easier?

THE METRIC SYSTEM VS. THE U.S. CUSTOMARY SYSTEM

Consequences and Implications

A3   What are the implications of the United States being the only country that has not officially converted to the metric system? Justify your answer.

_____

_____

_____

_____

_____

Cause and Effect

A2   What caused the French to adopt the metric system after the French Revolution? Support your answer.

_____

_____

_____

_____

_____

Sequencing

A1   List the elements of the metric system and the U.S. customary system in the order in which they were discussed in the text.

_____

_____

_____

_____

_____

_____

Main Idea, Theme, or Concept

C3 Theme: Does the overall theme of the text support the use of the U.S. customary system? Why or why not?

_____

_____

_____

_____

_____

Inference

C2 What inferences can be made from the chart in Figure 1? Support your answer with details from the text.

_____

_____

_____

_____

_____

Literary Elements

C1 Imagine a conversation between an American and a French person about the use of the metric system vs. the customary system. Choose one character from this scenario. Describe your chosen character's point of view on this topic. Use details to support your description.

_____

_____

_____

_____

_____

_____

_____

PGIL2025USA

Jacob's Ladder
Reading Comprehension Program

Program

Second Edition

Grade 4

Student Workbook
Nonfiction

Contributing Editors:
Joyce VanTassel-Baska,
Tamra Stambaugh,
Kimberley L. Chandler

Contributing Authors:
Heather French,
Paula Ginsburgh,
Tamra Stambaugh,
Joyce VanTassel-Baska

William & Mary
School of Education
CENTER FOR GIFTED EDUCATION

William & Mary
School of Education
Center for Gifted Education
P.O. Box 8795
Williamsburg, VA 23187

First published in 2017 by Prufrock Press Inc.

Published 2021 by Routledge
605 Third Avenue, New York, NY 10017
2 Park Square, Milton Park, Abingdon, Oxon OX14 4RN

Routledge is an imprint of the Taylor & Francis Group, an informa business

Edited by Lacy Compton

Cover and layout design by Raquel Trevino

ISBN-13: 978-1-61821-735-6

NEW YORK AND LONDON

Table of Contents

The American Revolutionary War

In 1765, Americans still considered themselves loyal subjects to the British crown. Great Britain had just finished the Seven Years War with France, during which the Americans helped the British defeat the French on American soil. After the war ended, Great Britain was looking for a way to help pay for the war. Because part of the reason they went to war with France was to protect their colonies in America, the British government decided to pay for the war through taxing Americans. The taxes implemented by the British government were not necessarily high. However, Americans were upset that they were not consulted about the new taxes. The Americans felt it was illegal, or at the very least not fair, to tax them without giving them proper representation within the British parliament. The statement "No taxation without representation" became a well-known phrase during the American Revolutionary War.

The first direct tax against the colonies was the Stamp Act in 1765. The Stamp Act declared that all official documents, newspapers, almanacs, pamphlets, and even playing cards must have official stamps on them. If they did not have stamps, which Americans must buy from Britain, then fines would be charged. Later acts further restricted the activities of Americans. The Currency Act prohibited Americans from printing their own paper money, which hindered trade among the colonies. The Quartering Act mandated that American colonists house British soldiers in their homes, which invaded the colonists' privacy. Colonists began voicing their protests against these taxes and acts. In 1770, the Boston Massacre occurred in Massachusetts. In protest of the Stamp Act and the Tea Act, colonists dumped tea bricks from British ships into Boston Harbor, in what is now known as the Boston Tea Party. During this protest, five Americans were killed.

Because of incidents like this one, as well as philosophical differences between England and the colonies, and America's desire for independence, the American Revolutionary War, also known as the American War of Independence, began in 1775.

In 1776, representatives from each of the 13 colonies met in Philadelphia where they unanimously signed the Declaration of Independence, thereby forming the United States of America. In 1778, the colonists formed an alliance with France. The French helped by sending money, munitions, and troops. These contributions from France helped level the playing field in

the war against Britain. However, the Americans were fighting against a monarchy for the right to establish a democracy. Even though France was helping them win their independence, Americans did not view France as a role model.

During the war, only 1/3 of the colonists, known as Patriots, supported war with Britain, 1/3 of colonists, known as Loyalists, remained loyal to Britain, and 1/3 of colonists remained neutral. However, throughout the war, the Patriots maintained control over 80%–90% of the land. The British were able to capture only a few coastal cities, which they gained through their strong Navy presence.

At the Battle at Saratoga in 1777, one of Britain's main armies was captured, the beginning of the end for the British. In 1781, the British army surrendered at the Battle of Yorktown. This surrender led to the signing of the Treaty of Paris for peace in 1783.

THE AMERICAN REVOLUTIONARY WAR

Main Idea, Theme, or Concept

C3 Concept: What concept represents why the American Revolutionary War was fought? State your answer in five words or less.

_____

_____

_____

Inference

C2 What inferences can be made about the French becoming allies with the Americans during the American Revolutionary War? Justify your answer.

_____

_____

_____

_____

Literary Elements

C1 Choose to be a Patriot, a Loyalist, or a neutral colonist. Describe your character's point of view regarding the war. Support your answer with details.

_____

_____

_____

_____

_____

_____

_____

_____

_____

Creative Synthesis

D3 Write a letter to your family about the American Revolutionary War from the point of view of a colonist, a British soldier, or a French soldier. Be sure to include enough details for the recipient of your letter to understand the war from your point of view.

_____

_____

_____

_____

_____

_____

_____

_____

Summarizing

D2 In three sentences or fewer, summarize the cause(s) of the American Revolutionary War.

_____

_____

_____

_____

Paraphrasing

D1 In your own words, rewrite the following statements:

"No taxation without representation."

_____

"Even though France was helping them win their independence, Americans did not view France as a role model."

_____

_____

The Exploration of Space

The exploration of space gives scientists the opportunity to learn about the sun, stars, and planets. Some space exploration involves scientists called *astronauts* traveling into space. Astronauts use spacecraft, such as space shuttles, to travel beyond the Earth's atmosphere into outer space, which begins about 60 miles above sea level. While in outer space, astronauts explore their surroundings with various tools, such as safety tethering systems to keep their spacesuits attached to the spacecraft (and smaller tethers to attach their tools to their spacesuits). Astronauts might also wear a SAFER or Simplified Aid for EVA Rescue (EVA stands for extravehicular activity, another term for spacewalk). A SAFER is like a backpack that uses small jet thrusters to allow an astronaut to move in space. Other space exploration does not require astronauts but instead uses spacecraft with robots or other mechanical devices, such as satellites, to gather information.

In order for spacecraft, manned or unmanned, to travel into outer space, they must first overcome the pull of Earth's gravity. The heavier an object, the more power is required to break the Earth's gravitational pull. As you can imagine, it takes a tremendous amount of power to launch a space shuttle. These large spacecraft require booster rockets full of fuel to launch them. The boosters burn the fuel that gives off gas bursts that push the spacecraft into the air. The spacecraft eventually reaches a height where the Earth's gravitational pull no longer affects it. Once it passes this point, the shuttle only needs to fire rockets to increase its speed or to change directions.

When a spacecraft is ready to return to Earth, it must first slow down. Once it reenters the atmosphere, it slows down considerably and begins falling toward Earth. The spacecraft deploys, or puts into action, parachutes that further slow down its descent. Spacecraft like space shuttles land on runways just like airplanes. Some of the earlier U.S. spacecraft "splashed down" in the ocean where the astronauts were picked up by boats.

On October 4, 1957, the Soviet Union launched Sputnik, a satellite that orbited Earth, and space exploration officially began. Years later, on April 12, 1961, Yuri A. Gagarin, a Soviet cosmonaut, became the first person to travel to space. In December 1968, the U.S. took the first trip to the moon in

the spacecraft Apollo 8, orbiting the moon 10 times before returning to Earth. Less than a year later, the American astronaut Neil Armstrong became the first person to walk on the moon on July 20, 1969. As Armstrong placed the American flag on the moon, he said, "That's one small step for a man, one giant leap for mankind."

Since this historic landing on the moon, astronauts have continued to explore space by traveling there and by studying the data collected by satellites and other unmanned spacecraft. Through space exploration, astronauts and scientists have learned and continue to learn much about the universe beyond Earth.

THE EXPLORATION OF SPACE

Consequences and Implications

A3 What are the implications of space exploration? Support your answer.

_____

_____

_____

_____

_____

_____

Cause and Effect

A2 What is the effect of the Earth's gravitational pull on spacecraft during launch? During reentry? Support your answer with evidence from the text.

_____

_____

_____

_____

_____

Sequencing

A1 In the space below, create a timeline of the history of space exploration as presented in the text.

Creative Synthesis

D3 Imagine you are an astronaut on the Apollo 8 spacecraft. Write a letter home describing the experience. Be sure to include plenty of details so the recipient of your letter feels like he or she was there with you.

_____

_____

_____

_____

_____

_____

_____

Summarizing

D2 In three sentences or fewer, describe the different ways scientists and astronauts explore space.

_____

_____

_____

_____

_____

_____

Paraphrasing

D1 In your own words, explain what Neil Armstrong meant when he said, "That's one small step for a man, one giant leap for mankind."

_____

_____

_____

_____

_____

_____

_____

Graphic Ice Cream

Tim and Lauren, the owners of Crema, an ice cream shop in Raleigh, NC, surveyed their customers about their favorite ice cream flavors, gathered information about the number of customers on each day of the week, and asked their employees to keep track of how they spend their work hours. They then used different kinds of graphs to represent these data.

Over the period of one month, the Crema owners asked their customers to choose their favorite flavors from a list including chocolate, vanilla, strawberry, banana toffee, strawberry cheesecake, blueberry almond, chocolate raspberry, coffee almond, peach pecan, and caramel pecan. The results are presented in Table 1.

Table 1

Customers' Favorite Flavors

Ice Cream Flavor	Number of Customers' Favorite Flavor
Chocolate	120
Vanilla	65
Strawberry	85
Banana Toffee	190
Strawberry Cheesecake	275
Blueberry Almond	135
Chocolate Raspberry	200
Coffee Almond	95
Peach Pecan	150
Caramel Pecan	75

Tim and Lauren then decided to graph the data they had gathered from their customers. They chose to graph the favorite flavors on a bar graph. A bar graph shows the relationships between groups. On a bar graph, one bar is not affected by another. Bar graphs are a good way to show large differences in results from surveys. They also are excellent tools for determining trends. By using a bar graph to represent the data about customers' favorite flavors, Lauren and Tim will be better able to plan their purchases of ingredients. They will know which ingredients will be used more quickly based on the flavor preferences. The bar graph of Crema customers' favorite flavors is presented in Figure 1.

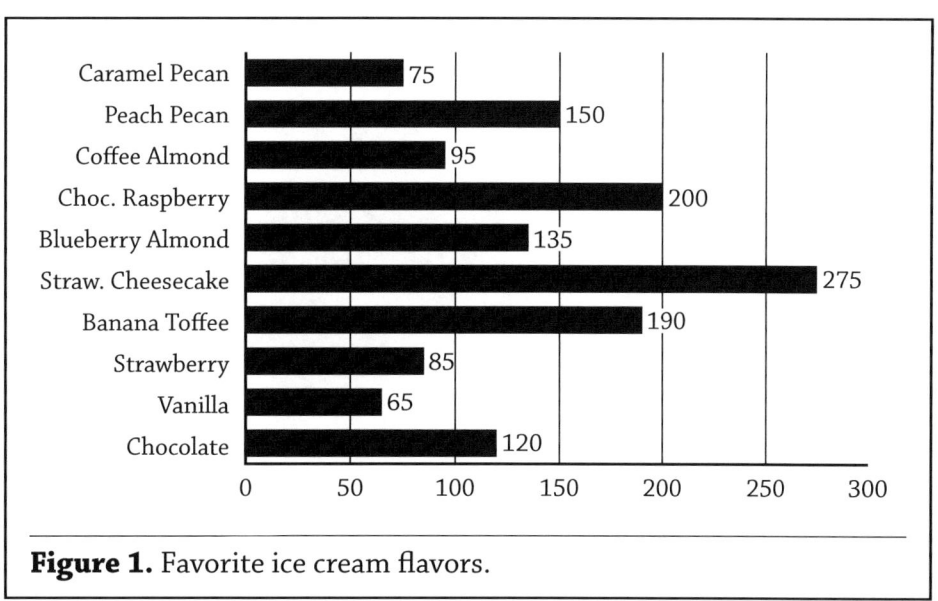

Figure 1. Favorite ice cream flavors.

After realizing how data can help them run their business more efficiently, Tim and Lauren decided to keep track of the number of customers coming to Crema on each day of the week. They were especially interested in Saturday and Sunday. They often wondered if they made or lost money by being open on the weekend. The results of their tracking are presented in Table 2.

Table 2
Number of Customers by Day

Day of the Week	Number of Customers
Monday	95
Tuesday	105
Wednesday	165
Thursday	210
Friday	275
Saturday	150
Sunday	45

Because the bar graph was helpful with comparing favorite flavors, the Crema owners decided to graph these data about customer attendance, too. However, instead of a bar graph, they chose to use a line graph. Line graphs track continuing data where one point is affected by another. With line graphs, there are points on a graph with x- and y-axis coordinates. Points are then joined by a line. Line graphs often are used to track rainfall, the average daily temperature, or, in the case of Crema, the daily number of customers. The line graph they used is presented in Figure 2.

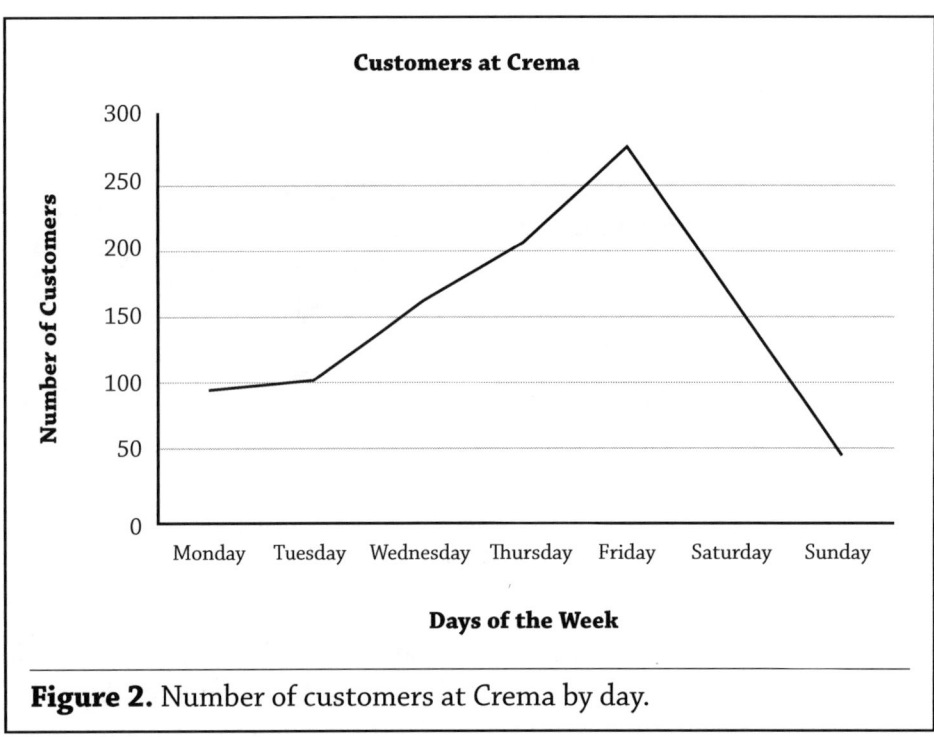

Figure 2. Number of customers at Crema by day.

Tim and Lauren analyzed the data to determine on what days they were most profitable. As they were thinking about money, they wondered how productive their employees were. They decided to ask their employees to keep track of how they spent their work hours. The results of this tracking are presented in Table 3.

Table 3

How Crema Employees Spend a Total Work Day (12 Hours)

Chore	Hours	Percentage of Work Day
Preparing Store to Open	1	8%
Taking Orders	3.5	30%
Preparing Orders	5	42%
Completing Transactions	1	8%
Reconciling Register	.5	4%
Closing	1	8%

The owners of Crema decided to use a circle, or pie, graph to display the data gathered from their employees. Pie graphs are particularly helpful when looking at how a part relates to a whole. In this case, Tim and Lauren wanted to see how the time spent on each chore related to the work day as a whole. The pie chart is presented in Figure 3.

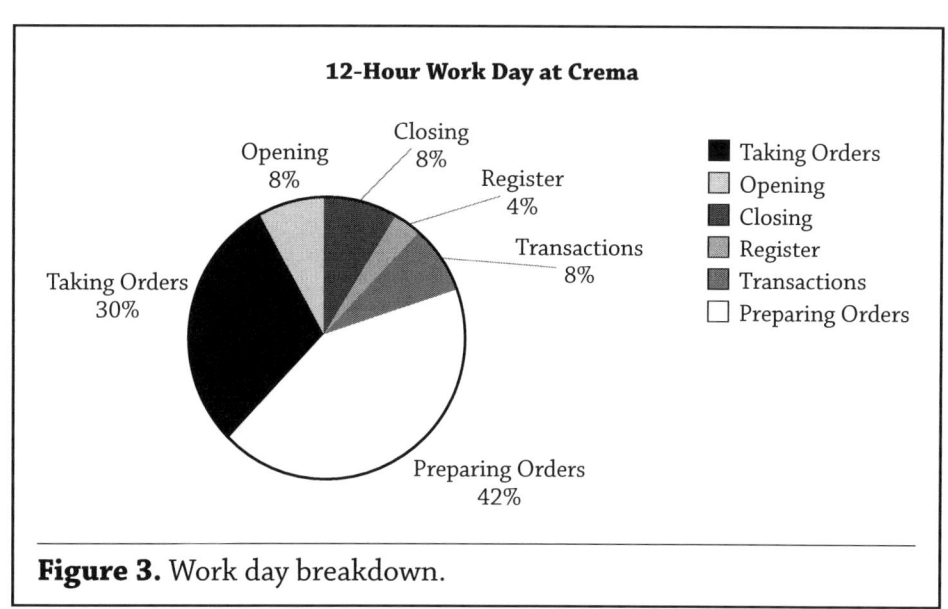

Figure 3. Work day breakdown.

GRAPHIC ICE CREAM

Generalizations

B3 Write at least three generalizations about using graphs to represent data.

_____

_____

_____

_____

Classifications

B2 Look at your list of details. Classify your list into the categories of bar, line, or pie graphs based on which type of graph would be most appropriate for each type of data. Use the definitions from the text to make your classification decisions.

_____

_____

_____

_____

Details

B1 List 15–20 different kinds of data that are often gathered or that could be gathered.

_____

_____

_____

_____

_____

_____

_____

Main Idea, Theme, or Concept

C3   Main Idea: Why did the author title this selection "Graphic Ice Cream"? Use evidence from the text to support your answer.

_____

_____

_____

_____

_____

Inference

C2   What inferences can you draw based on:
- the data and graph about customers' favorite flavors?
- the data and graph about daily customer counts?
- the data and graph about the use of employees' work hours?

_____

_____

_____

_____

_____

_____

Literary Elements

C1   How would you characterize the owners of Crema? Using details from the text to support your answer, describe the kind of business owners they are.

_____

_____

_____

_____

_____

_____

_____

The Great Depression

The Great Depression began in the United States with the stock market crash of 1929. The Depression quickly spread throughout Europe and then the rest of the world.

Economists are divided over what caused the Great Depression. Some believe that at the end of the post-World War I building boom, consumer goods were flooding the market. The supply of goods was far exceeding demand, which caused the economic system to collapse. Others believe that it was a simple case of too many banks playing the stock market with depositors' money. A third theory contends that the Depression deepened because so many people were carrying debt before the crash, and when the crash occurred they simply stopped spending money, which crippled the capitalist market. Another theory blames the severity of the Depression on the extreme drought that struck the Midwest agricultural business during the summer of 1930. Finally, a fifth theory states that it was the collapse of foreign banks that took with it a large amount of U.S. wealth and destroyed the prospect of world trade that caused the Depression to become a Great Depression.

Regardless of the cause, the Great Depression was one of the saddest periods in U.S. history. During this time period from 1929 to 1941, Americans endured much hardship. In the Midwest, farmers experienced an intense drought that earned this agricultural area the name "Dust Bowl." During the summer of 1930, many Midwest farmers were forced to leave their lands because of dust storms that blew much of the soil away. The dust storms were caused by a failure to rotate crops and the exposure of soil by the removal of grass through plowing. With the drought, the soil dried out, became dust, and then blew away in black clouds. Much of the soil was lost in the Atlantic Ocean as it blew eastward. Many people in the Midwest suffered from dust pneumonia and malnutrition.

In other areas of the country, conditions were not any better. Unemployment rose from 5 million people without jobs in 1930 to 11 million people without jobs in 1931. A staggering 25% of Americans were unemployed. Many people lost their homes. Sadly, 20% of children were hungry and did not have proper clothing or houses. Many schools closed because they could not afford to stay open. Of young people between the ages of 16 and 24, 40% of them were neither in school nor working. Children wrote letters to the First Lady, Eleanor Roosevelt, begging her to help them find food, clothing, and shelter.

After his inauguration in 1933, President Franklin D. Roosevelt passed the New Deal legislation. The New Deal restructured the economy and increased government spending to stimulate demand within the market, create jobs, and provide relief for the poor and unemployed. However, in 1937, the American economy took another nosedive that further deepened the Great Depression. During the period of the Depression, most countries experienced political upheaval that allowed dictators like Hitler, Stalin, and Mussolini to rise to power, leading to the beginning of World War II in 1939.

Supplying materials and resources for troops to protect the world against Nazi Germany stimulated economies in Europe from 1937–1939, pulling these nations out of depression. In the U.S., jobs increased, people worked overtime to make up for lost wages, and Americans agreed to rations for the first time in support of the war effort. The President pushed for a large quantity of war supplies no matter what it cost the government. In the United States, the Great Depression ended in 1941 when America entered World War II.

THE GREAT DEPRESSION

Consequences and Implications

A3 What were the consequences of the Great Depression for children? Justify your answer with supporting details.

_____

_____

_____

Cause and Effect

A2 What caused the end of the Great Depression in Europe? In America? Support your answer.

_____

_____

_____

_____

_____

_____

Sequencing

A1 List, in order, the events of the Great Depression as discussed in the text.

_____

_____

_____

_____

_____

_____

_____

_____

Generalizations

B3 Write at least three generalizations about your life today compared to the life of a child during the Great Depression.

_____

_____

_____

_____

Classifications

B2 Study your list. Classify your details into categories. You may not have a "miscellaneous" or "other" category.

_____

_____

_____

_____

_____

_____

_____

_____

Details

B1 List at least 25 things and/or privileges that you have today that you would not have had growing up during the Great Depression.

_____

_____

_____

_____

_____

_____

_____

_____

_____

It's Electric!

How much do you know about electricity? Electricity refers to the movement of charged particles within atoms. There are two kinds of charged particles: Electrons have a negative charge, and protons have a positive charge. Electrons are constantly orbiting the nucleus of an atom. When an electromotive force is applied through an energy source such as a battery or an outlet, the electrons will jump from nucleus to nucleus along the path of the force.

The rate at which electrons move is called *current*. Current is affected by resistance, which is related to the physical properties of the material through which electrons are moving. In materials with low resistance, like copper wire, electrons are easily persuaded to leave their original nucleus and travel to the next nucleus. Copper wire is a good conductor because electrons are easily conducted, or moved, along the path of the applied electromotive force. High resistance materials, such as rubber, make it nearly impossible for electrons to move from nucleus to nucleus. Rubber does not conduct electrons along the path of applied force. Because it does not allow conduction, rubber is called an *insulator*.

Another type of electricity is static electricity. With static electricity, the electrical particles are not moving; instead a charge has built up in something, like your body after rubbing your feet on carpet. When you rub your feet on the carpet, electrons are transferred from one object to the other. One object, either your feet or the carpet, ends up with extra electrons and a negative charge while the other object is positively charged because it has more protons. For the purposes of this example, let's say your feet are negatively charged and the carpet is positively charged. Then, you touch a neutral object, such as a doorknob, and experience a shock. The shock is actually a tiny lightning bolt that occurs when the extra negatively charged electrons are transferred to the neutrally charged doorknob. The electrons in your body are attracted to the protons in the doorknob and "jump" toward them. At the same time, the electrons already in the doorknob move as far away from the new electrons as possible. In the case of electricity, opposites attract.

Ancient Greeks were familiar with static electricity. They discovered the shocking characteristics of jumping electrons when they rubbed objects on fur. However, moving electricity produced by the application of an electro-

motive force was not discovered until much later. Many people believe Benjamin Franklin discovered electricity. Although this point is debatable, it can be said without doubt that Benjamin Franklin discovered that lightning is a form of electricity through his famous kite-flying experiment. In this experiment, Franklin tied a key to the end of a wet kite string. Then, he flew the kite during a lightning storm. When the lightning struck the key, he felt a spark on his finger and he knew that lightning was a form of electricity.

Thomas Edison is known as the inventor who was first able to capture electricity to produce light. He invented the light bulb and first demonstrated this invention on December 31, 1879 in Menlo Park, NJ. During this demonstration, he said, "We will make electricity so cheap that only the rich will burn candles."

Today, electricity is everywhere. There are lights in our houses, our schools, along our streets, and in our cars. Electricity even runs through our computers, our car engines, our televisions, our radios, and our video games.

IT'S ELECTRIC!

Generalizations

B3 Based on your list and your classifications, write at least three generalizations about the use of electricity.

_____

_____

_____

_____

Classifications

B2 Look at your list of examples. Classify each example into categories. You may not have a "miscellaneous" or "other" category.

_____

_____

_____

_____

Details

B1 List as many examples of the use of electricity as you can in 2 minutes. (You should have at least 25 examples.)

_____

_____

_____

_____

_____

_____

_____

_____

_____

_____

Creative Synthesis

D3   Invent a new way to use electricity. Create an advertisement to sell your new invention to an audience of your choice (your classmates, your teachers, your parents, your city, or another audience). You may use illustrations.

Summarizing

D2   In five sentences or fewer, summarize what happens when you rub your feet on the carpet and then touch a doorknob.

_____

_____

_____

_____

_____

Paraphrasing

D1   In your own words, restate what Thomas Edison meant when he said, "We will make electricity so cheap that only the rich will burn candles."

_____

_____

_____

_____

_____

The Metric System vs. the U.S. Customary System

The metric system and the U.S. customary system are both systems of measurement. So, what is the difference between them and why are there two different systems? In today's global society, wouldn't it be easier if the whole world used the same system?

Elements of the metric system date back to the reign of Louis XVI in France during the 18th century. In 1791, after the French Revolution, the metric system was adopted by the French as the official system of measurement. The goals of the new metric system were to develop a single unit for physical quantity and to create a measurement system that did not require the use of conversion factors. Specifically, all measurements of length are in meters, measurements of liquid are in liters, and measurements of weight are in grams. All three types of measurement use a common set of prefixes that are related to each other by powers of 10. For example, a decameter is 10 meters, a hectometer is 100 meters, and a kilometer is 1,000 meters. Conversely, a decimeter is 1/10 of a meter, a centimeter is 1/100 of a meter, and millimeter is 1/1000 of a meter. There are no conversion factors required to switch among these different representations of the measurement of length. Time is the only unit of measurement that is not unified by the metric system. Time still requires conversion factors to switch among days, hours, minutes, and seconds.

The U.S. customary system can be traced back to the Roman system of measurement. It is based on the Imperial System, which was used by Great Britain until 1995. Today, the United States is the only country that has not converted to the metric system from the customary system, even though the Omnibus Trade and Competitiveness Act of 1988 stated that the metric system is the preferred system for industry and trade. In the United States, the metric system is most commonly used by the military, medical field, and scientific realms. The customary system is used in most other instances. The customary system measures length in inches, feet, yards, and miles; measures general volume in cubic inches, cubic feet, and cubic yards; measures liquid volume in fluid ounces, cups, pints, quarts and gallons; and measures weight in ounces, pounds, and tons. The customary system requires conversion factors to convert

Customary System			Metric System		
From	Multiply by	To get	From	Multiply by	To get
feet	12	inches	kilometers	1000	meters
pounds	16	ounces	grams	1000	milligrams
quarts	4	cups	liters	10	deciliters

Figure 1. Converting units in the customary system vs. the metric system.

units. For example, to convert feet into yards, you must know that there are 3 feet in one yard. You then would divide the total number of feet by three to determine the total number of yards. Similarly, to convert cups into quarts, you have to know that there are 4 cups in a quart.

The chart in Figure 1 shows the conversion factors needed for the customary system compared to conversion of measurement units within the metric system.

Which system do you think is easier?

THE METRIC SYSTEM VS. THE U.S. CUSTOMARY SYSTEM

Consequences and Implications

A3 What are the implications of the United States being the only country that has not officially converted to the metric system? Justify your answer.

_____

_____

_____

_____

_____

Cause and Effect

A2 What caused the French to adopt the metric system after the French Revolution? Support your answer.

_____

_____

_____

_____

_____

Sequencing

A1 List the elements of the metric system and the U.S. customary system in the order in which they were discussed in the text.

_____

_____

_____

_____

_____

_____

_____

Main Idea, Theme, or Concept

C3   Theme: Does the overall theme of the text support the use of the U.S. customary system? Why or why not?

_____

_____

_____

_____

_____

Inference

C2   What inferences can be made from the chart in Figure 1? Support your answer with details from the text.

_____

_____

_____

_____

_____

Literary Elements

C1   Imagine a conversation between an American and a French person about the use of the metric system vs. the customary system. Choose one character from this scenario. Describe your chosen character's point of view on this topic. Use details to support your description.

_____

_____

_____

_____

_____

_____

_____

_____

For Product Safety Concerns and Information, please contact our EU representative: GPSR@taylorandfrancis.com Taylor & Francis Verlag GmbH, Kaufingerstraße 24, 80331 München, Germany.

Jacob's Ladder
Reading Comprehension Program

Reading Comprehension Program

Second Edition

Grade

4

Student Workbook Nonfiction

Contributing Editors:
Joyce VanTassel-Baska,
Tamra Stambaugh,
Kimberley L. Chandler

Contributing Authors:
Heather French,
Paula Ginsburgh,
Tamra Stambaugh,
Joyce VanTassel-Baska

William & Mary
School of Education
CENTER FOR GIFTED EDUCATION

William & Mary
School of Education
Center for Gifted Education
P.O. Box 8795
Williamsburg, VA 23187

First published in 2017 by Prufrock Press Inc.

Published 2021 by Routledge
605 Third Avenue, New York, NY 10017
2 Park Square, Milton Park, Abingdon, Oxon OX14 4RN

Routledge is an imprint of the Taylor & Francis Group, an informa business

Edited by Lacy Compton

Cover and layout design by Raquel Trevino

ISBN-13: 978-1-61821-735-6

NEW YORK AND LONDON

Table of Contents

The American Revolutionary War

In 1765, Americans still considered themselves loyal subjects to the British crown. Great Britain had just finished the Seven Years War with France, during which the Americans helped the British defeat the French on American soil. After the war ended, Great Britain was looking for a way to help pay for the war. Because part of the reason they went to war with France was to protect their colonies in America, the British government decided to pay for the war through taxing Americans. The taxes implemented by the British government were not necessarily high. However, Americans were upset that they were not consulted about the new taxes. The Americans felt it was illegal, or at the very least not fair, to tax them without giving them proper representation within the British parliament. The statement "No taxation without representation" became a well-known phrase during the American Revolutionary War.

The first direct tax against the colonies was the Stamp Act in 1765. The Stamp Act declared that all official documents, newspapers, almanacs, pamphlets, and even playing cards must have official stamps on them. If they did not have stamps, which Americans must buy from Britain, then fines would be charged. Later acts further restricted the activities of Americans. The Currency Act prohibited Americans from printing their own paper money, which hindered trade among the colonies. The Quartering Act mandated that American colonists house British soldiers in their homes, which invaded the colonists' privacy. Colonists began voicing their protests against these taxes and acts. In 1770, the Boston Massacre occurred in Massachusetts. In protest of the Stamp Act and the Tea Act, colonists dumped tea bricks from British ships into Boston Harbor, in what is now known as the Boston Tea Party. During this protest, five Americans were killed.

Because of incidents like this one, as well as philosophical differences between England and the colonies, and America's desire for independence, the American Revolutionary War, also known as the American War of Independence, began in 1775.

In 1776, representatives from each of the 13 colonies met in Philadelphia where they unanimously signed the Declaration of Independence, thereby forming the United States of America. In 1778, the colonists formed an alliance with France. The French helped by sending money, munitions, and troops. These contributions from France helped level the playing field in

the war against Britain. However, the Americans were fighting against a monarchy for the right to establish a democracy. Even though France was helping them win their independence, Americans did not view France as a role model.

During the war, only 1/3 of the colonists, known as Patriots, supported war with Britain, 1/3 of colonists, known as Loyalists, remained loyal to Britain, and 1/3 of colonists remained neutral. However, throughout the war, the Patriots maintained control over 80%–90% of the land. The British were able to capture only a few coastal cities, which they gained through their strong Navy presence.

At the Battle at Saratoga in 1777, one of Britain's main armies was captured, the beginning of the end for the British. In 1781, the British army surrendered at the Battle of Yorktown. This surrender led to the signing of the Treaty of Paris for peace in 1783.

THE AMERICAN REVOLUTIONARY WAR

Main Idea, Theme, or Concept

C3 Concept: What concept represents why the American Revolutionary War was fought? State your answer in five words or less.

_____

_____

_____

Inference

C2 What inferences can be made about the French becoming allies with the Americans during the American Revolutionary War? Justify your answer.

_____

_____

_____

_____

Literary Elements

C1 Choose to be a Patriot, a Loyalist, or a neutral colonist. Describe your character's point of view regarding the war. Support your answer with details.

_____

_____

_____

_____

_____

_____

_____

Creative Synthesis

D3   Write a letter to your family about the American Revolutionary War from the point of view of a colonist, a British soldier, or a French soldier. Be sure to include enough details for the recipient of your letter to understand the war from your point of view.

_____

_____

_____

_____

_____

_____

_____

_____

Summarizing

D2   In three sentences or fewer, summarize the cause(s) of the American Revolutionary War.

_____

_____

_____

_____

Paraphrasing

D1   In your own words, rewrite the following statements:

"No taxation without representation."

_____

"Even though France was helping them win their independence, Americans did not view France as a role model."

_____

_____

The Exploration of Space

The exploration of space gives scientists the opportunity to learn about the sun, stars, and planets. Some space exploration involves scientists called *astronauts* traveling into space. Astronauts use spacecraft, such as space shuttles, to travel beyond the Earth's atmosphere into outer space, which begins about 60 miles above sea level. While in outer space, astronauts explore their surroundings with various tools, such as safety tethering systems to keep their spacesuits attached to the spacecraft (and smaller tethers to attach their tools to their spacesuits). Astronauts might also wear a SAFER or Simplified Aid for EVA Rescue (EVA stands for extravehicular activity, another term for spacewalk). A SAFER is like a backpack that uses small jet thrusters to allow an astronaut to move in space. Other space exploration does not require astronauts but instead uses spacecraft with robots or other mechanical devices, such as satellites, to gather information.

In order for spacecraft, manned or unmanned, to travel into outer space, they must first overcome the pull of Earth's gravity. The heavier an object, the more power is required to break the Earth's gravitational pull. As you can imagine, it takes a tremendous amount of power to launch a space shuttle. These large spacecraft require booster rockets full of fuel to launch them. The boosters burn the fuel that gives off gas bursts that push the spacecraft into the air. The spacecraft eventually reaches a height where the Earth's gravitational pull no longer affects it. Once it passes this point, the shuttle only needs to fire rockets to increase its speed or to change directions.

When a spacecraft is ready to return to Earth, it must first slow down. Once it reenters the atmosphere, it slows down considerably and begins falling toward Earth. The spacecraft deploys, or puts into action, parachutes that further slow down its descent. Spacecraft like space shuttles land on runways just like airplanes. Some of the earlier U.S. spacecraft "splashed down" in the ocean where the astronauts were picked up by boats.

On October 4, 1957, the Soviet Union launched Sputnik, a satellite that orbited Earth, and space exploration officially began. Years later, on April 12, 1961, Yuri A. Gagarin, a Soviet cosmonaut, became the first person to travel to space. In December 1968, the U.S. took the first trip to the moon in

the spacecraft Apollo 8, orbiting the moon 10 times before returning to Earth. Less than a year later, the American astronaut Neil Armstrong became the first person to walk on the moon on July 20, 1969. As Armstrong placed the American flag on the moon, he said, "That's one small step for a man, one giant leap for mankind."

Since this historic landing on the moon, astronauts have continued to explore space by traveling there and by studying the data collected by satellites and other unmanned spacecraft. Through space exploration, astronauts and scientists have learned and continue to learn much about the universe beyond Earth.

THE EXPLORATION OF SPACE

Consequences and Implications

A3 What are the implications of space exploration? Support your answer.

_____

_____

_____

_____

_____

_____

_____

Cause and Effect

A2 What is the effect of the Earth's gravitational pull on spacecraft during launch? During reentry? Support your answer with evidence from the text.

_____

_____

_____

_____

_____

_____

Sequencing

A1 In the space below, create a timeline of the history of space exploration as presented in the text.

Creative Synthesis

D3 Imagine you are an astronaut on the Apollo 8 spacecraft. Write a letter home describing the experience. Be sure to include plenty of details so the recipient of your letter feels like he or she was there with you.

_____

_____

_____

_____

_____

_____

_____

Summarizing

D2 In three sentences or fewer, describe the different ways scientists and astronauts explore space.

_____

_____

_____

_____

_____

_____

Paraphrasing

D1 In your own words, explain what Neil Armstrong meant when he said, "That's one small step for a man, one giant leap for mankind."

_____

_____

_____

_____

_____

_____

Graphic Ice Cream

Tim and Lauren, the owners of Crema, an ice cream shop in Raleigh, NC, surveyed their customers about their favorite ice cream flavors, gathered information about the number of customers on each day of the week, and asked their employees to keep track of how they spend their work hours. They then used different kinds of graphs to represent these data.

Over the period of one month, the Crema owners asked their customers to choose their favorite flavors from a list including chocolate, vanilla, strawberry, banana toffee, strawberry cheesecake, blueberry almond, chocolate raspberry, coffee almond, peach pecan, and caramel pecan. The results are presented in Table 1.

Table 1

Customers' Favorite Flavors

Ice Cream Flavor	Number of Customers' Favorite Flavor
Chocolate	120
Vanilla	65
Strawberry	85
Banana Toffee	190
Strawberry Cheesecake	275
Blueberry Almond	135
Chocolate Raspberry	200
Coffee Almond	95
Peach Pecan	150
Caramel Pecan	75

Tim and Lauren then decided to graph the data they had gathered from their customers. They chose to graph the favorite flavors on a bar graph. A bar graph shows the relationships between groups. On a bar graph, one bar is not affected by another. Bar graphs are a good way to show large differences in results from surveys. They also are excellent tools for determining trends. By using a bar graph to represent the data about customers' favorite flavors, Lauren and Tim will be better able to plan their purchases of ingredients. They will know which ingredients will be used more quickly based on the flavor preferences. The bar graph of Crema customers' favorite flavors is presented in Figure 1.

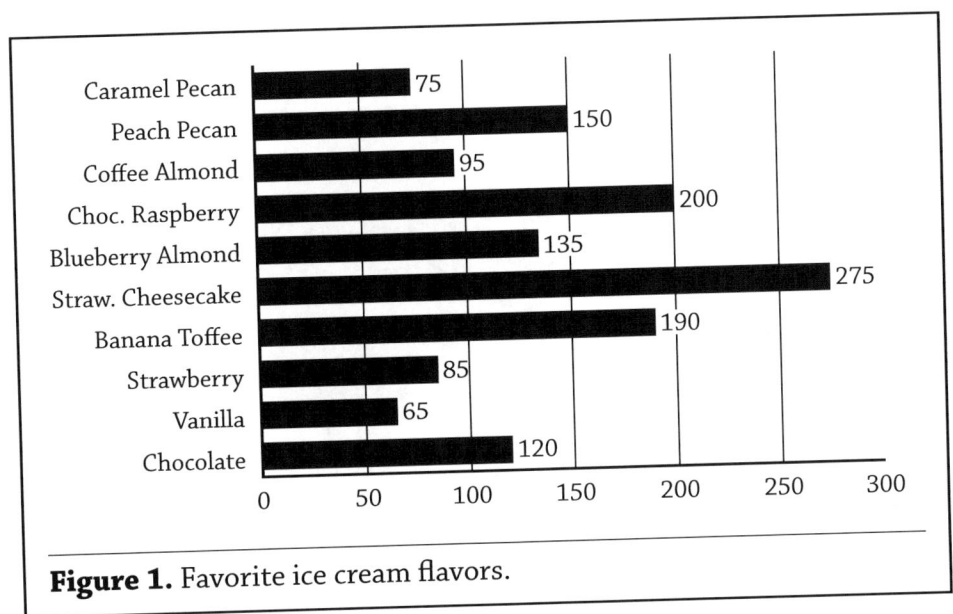

Figure 1. Favorite ice cream flavors.

After realizing how data can help them run their business more efficiently, Tim and Lauren decided to keep track of the number of customers coming to Crema on each day of the week. They were especially interested in Saturday and Sunday. They often wondered if they made or lost money by being open on the weekend. The results of their tracking are presented in Table 2.

Table 2

Number of Customers by Day

Day of the Week	Number of Customers
Monday	95
Tuesday	105
Wednesday	165
Thursday	210
Friday	275
Saturday	150
Sunday	45

Because the bar graph was helpful with comparing favorite flavors, the Crema owners decided to graph these data about customer attendance, too. However, instead of a bar graph, they chose to use a line graph. Line graphs track continuing data where one point is affected by another. With line graphs, there are points on a graph with x- and y-axis coordinates. Points are then joined by a line. Line graphs often are used to track rainfall, the average daily temperature, or, in the case of Crema, the daily number of customers. The line graph they used is presented in Figure 2.

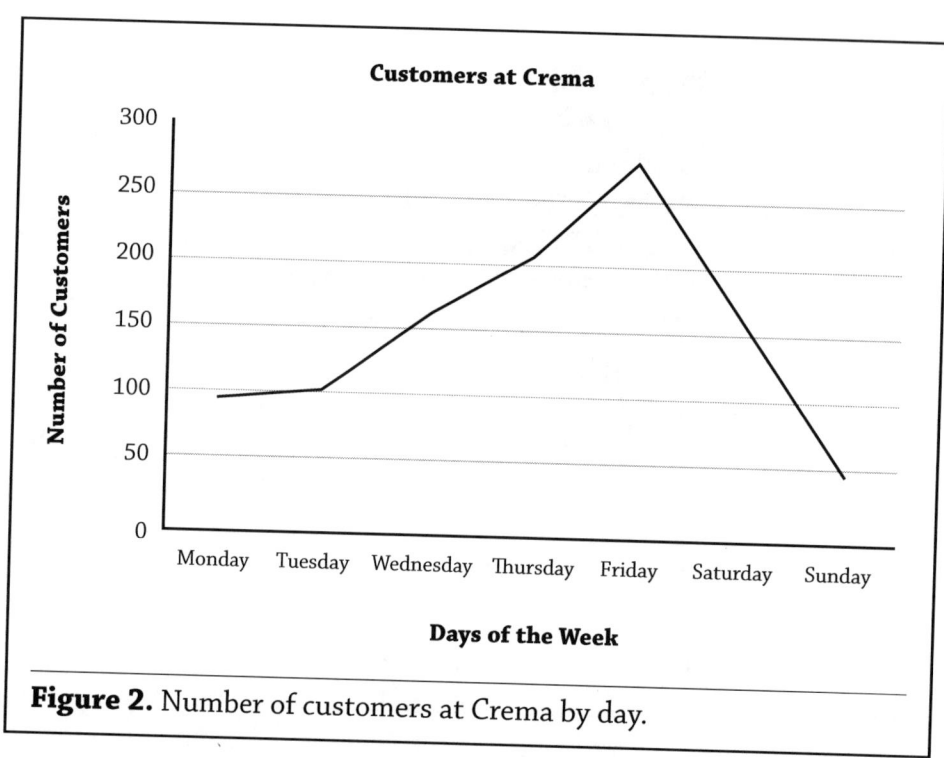

Figure 2. Number of customers at Crema by day.

Tim and Lauren analyzed the data to determine on what days they were most profitable. As they were thinking about money, they wondered how productive their employees were. They decided to ask their employees to keep track of how they spent their work hours. The results of this tracking are presented in Table 3.

Table 3

How Crema Employees Spend a Total Work Day (12 Hours)

Chore	Hours	Percentage of Work Day
Preparing Store to Open	1	8%
Taking Orders	3.5	30%
Preparing Orders	5	42%
Completing Transactions	1	8%
Reconciling Register	.5	4%
Closing	1	8%

The owners of Crema decided to use a circle, or pie, graph to display the data gathered from their employees. Pie graphs are particularly helpful when looking at how a part relates to a whole. In this case, Tim and Lauren wanted to see how the time spent on each chore related to the work day as a whole. The pie chart is presented in Figure 3.

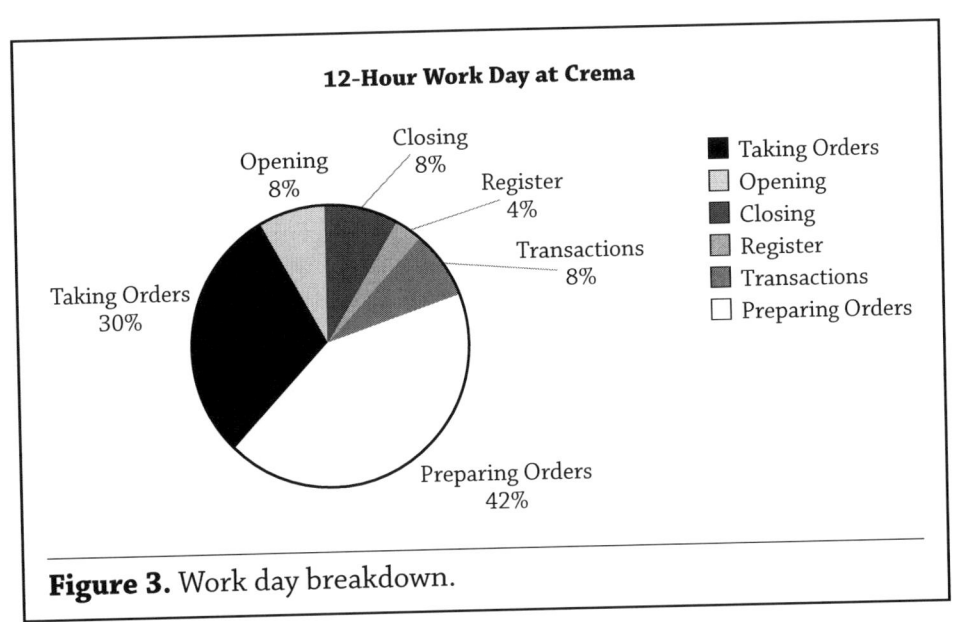

Figure 3. Work day breakdown.

GRAPHIC ICE CREAM

Generalizations

B3 Write at least three generalizations about using graphs to represent data.

_____

_____

_____

_____

Classifications

B2 Look at your list of details. Classify your list into the categories of bar, line, or pie graphs based on which type of graph would be most appropriate for each type of data. Use the definitions from the text to make your classification decisions.

_____

_____

_____

_____

_____

Details

B1 List 15–20 different kinds of data that are often gathered or that could be gathered.

_____

_____

_____

_____

_____

_____

_____

_____

_____

Main Idea, Theme, or Concept

C3 Main Idea: Why did the author title this selection "Graphic Ice Cream"? Use evidence from the text to support your answer.

_____

_____

_____

_____

_____

Inference

C2 What inferences can you draw based on:
- the data and graph about customers' favorite flavors?
- the data and graph about daily customer counts?
- the data and graph about the use of employees' work hours?

_____

_____

_____

_____

_____

_____

Literary Elements

C1 How would you characterize the owners of Crema? Using details from the text to support your answer, describe the kind of business owners they are.

_____

_____

_____

_____

_____

_____

The Great Depression

The Great Depression began in the United States with the stock market crash of 1929. The Depression quickly spread throughout Europe and then the rest of the world.

Economists are divided over what caused the Great Depression. Some believe that at the end of the post-World War I building boom, consumer goods were flooding the market. The supply of goods was far exceeding demand, which caused the economic system to collapse. Others believe that it was a simple case of too many banks playing the stock market with depositors' money. A third theory contends that the Depression deepened because so many people were carrying debt before the crash, and when the crash occurred they simply stopped spending money, which crippled the capitalist market. Another theory blames the severity of the Depression on the extreme drought that struck the Midwest agricultural business during the summer of 1930. Finally, a fifth theory states that it was the collapse of foreign banks that took with it a large amount of U.S. wealth and destroyed the prospect of world trade that caused the Depression to become a Great Depression.

Regardless of the cause, the Great Depression was one of the saddest periods in U.S. history. During this time period from 1929 to 1941, Americans endured much hardship. In the Midwest, farmers experienced an intense drought that earned this agricultural area the name "Dust Bowl." During the summer of 1930, many Midwest farmers were forced to leave their lands because of dust storms that blew much of the soil away. The dust storms were caused by a failure to rotate crops and the exposure of soil by the removal of grass through plowing. With the drought, the soil dried out, became dust, and then blew away in black clouds. Much of the soil was lost in the Atlantic Ocean as it blew eastward. Many people in the Midwest suffered from dust pneumonia and malnutrition.

In other areas of the country, conditions were not any better. Unemployment rose from 5 million people without jobs in 1930 to 11 million people without jobs in 1931. A staggering 25% of Americans were unemployed. Many people lost their homes. Sadly, 20% of children were hungry and did not have proper clothing or houses. Many schools closed because they could not afford to stay open. Of young people between the ages of 16 and 24, 40% of them were neither in school nor working. Children wrote letters to the First Lady, Eleanor Roosevelt, begging her to help them find food, clothing, and shelter.

After his inauguration in 1933, President Franklin D. Roosevelt passed the New Deal legislation. The New Deal restructured the economy and increased government spending to stimulate demand within the market, create jobs, and provide relief for the poor and unemployed. However, in 1937, the American economy took another nosedive that further deepened the Great Depression. During the period of the Depression, most countries experienced political upheaval that allowed dictators like Hitler, Stalin, and Mussolini to rise to power, leading to the beginning of World War II in 1939.

Supplying materials and resources for troops to protect the world against Nazi Germany stimulated economies in Europe from 1937–1939, pulling these nations out of depression. In the U.S., jobs increased, people worked overtime to make up for lost wages, and Americans agreed to rations for the first time in support of the war effort. The President pushed for a large quantity of war supplies no matter what it cost the government. In the United States, the Great Depression ended in 1941 when America entered World War II.

THE GREAT DEPRESSION

Consequences and Implications

A3 What were the consequences of the Great Depression for children? Justify your answer with supporting details.

_____

_____

_____

Cause and Effect

A2 What caused the end of the Great Depression in Europe? In America? Support your answer.

_____

_____

_____

_____

_____

_____

Sequencing

A1 List, in order, the events of the Great Depression as discussed in the text.

_____

_____

_____

_____

_____

_____

_____

_____

Generalizations

B3 Write at least three generalizations about your life today compared to the life of a child during the Great Depression.

_____

_____

_____

_____

Classifications

B2 Study your list. Classify your details into categories. You may not have a "miscellaneous" or "other" category.

_____

_____

_____

_____

_____

_____

_____

_____

Details

B1 List at least 25 things and/or privileges that you have today that you would not have had growing up during the Great Depression.

_____

_____

_____

_____

_____

_____

_____

_____

_____

It's Electric!

How much do you know about electricity? Electricity refers to the movement of charged particles within atoms. There are two kinds of charged particles: Electrons have a negative charge, and protons have a positive charge. Electrons are constantly orbiting the nucleus of an atom. When an electromotive force is applied through an energy source such as a battery or an outlet, the electrons will jump from nucleus to nucleus along the path of the force.

The rate at which electrons move is called *current*. Current is affected by resistance, which is related to the physical properties of the material through which electrons are moving. In materials with low resistance, like copper wire, electrons are easily persuaded to leave their original nucleus and travel to the next nucleus. Copper wire is a good conductor because electrons are easily conducted, or moved, along the path of the applied electromotive force. High resistance materials, such as rubber, make it nearly impossible for electrons to move from nucleus to nucleus. Rubber does not conduct electrons along the path of applied force. Because it does not allow conduction, rubber is called an *insulator*.

Another type of electricity is static electricity. With static electricity, the electrical particles are not moving; instead a charge has built up in something, like your body after rubbing your feet on carpet. When you rub your feet on the carpet, electrons are transferred from one object to the other. One object, either your feet or the carpet, ends up with extra electrons and a negative charge while the other object is positively charged because it has more protons. For the purposes of this example, let's say your feet are negatively charged and the carpet is positively charged. Then, you touch a neutral object, such as a doorknob, and experience a shock. The shock is actually a tiny lightning bolt that occurs when the extra negatively charged electrons are transferred to the neutrally charged doorknob. The electrons in your body are attracted to the protons in the doorknob and "jump" toward them. At the same time, the electrons already in the doorknob move as far away from the new electrons as possible. In the case of electricity, opposites attract.

Ancient Greeks were familiar with static electricity. They discovered the shocking characteristics of jumping electrons when they rubbed objects on fur. However, moving electricity produced by the application of an electro-

motive force was not discovered until much later. Many people believe Benjamin Franklin discovered electricity. Although this point is debatable, it can be said without doubt that Benjamin Franklin discovered that lightning is a form of electricity through his famous kite-flying experiment. In this experiment, Franklin tied a key to the end of a wet kite string. Then, he flew the kite during a lightning storm. When the lightning struck the key, he felt a spark on his finger and he knew that lightning was a form of electricity.

Thomas Edison is known as the inventor who was first able to capture electricity to produce light. He invented the light bulb and first demonstrated this invention on December 31, 1879 in Menlo Park, NJ. During this demonstration, he said, "We will make electricity so cheap that only the rich will burn candles."

Today, electricity is everywhere. There are lights in our houses, our schools, along our streets, and in our cars. Electricity even runs through our computers, our car engines, our televisions, our radios, and our video games.

IT'S ELECTRIC!

Generalizations

B3 Based on your list and your classifications, write at least three generalizations about the use of electricity.

_____

_____

_____

_____

Classifications

B2 Look at your list of examples. Classify each example into categories. You may not have a "miscellaneous" or "other" category.

_____

_____

_____

_____

Details

B1 List as many examples of the use of electricity as you can in 2 minutes. (You should have at least 25 examples.)

_____

_____

_____

_____

_____

_____

_____

_____

Creative Synthesis

D3 Invent a new way to use electricity. Create an advertisement to sell your new invention to an audience of your choice (your classmates, your teachers, your parents, your city, or another audience). You may use illustrations.

Summarizing

D2 In five sentences or fewer, summarize what happens when you rub your feet on the carpet and then touch a doorknob.

Paraphrasing

D1 In your own words, restate what Thomas Edison meant when he said, "We will make electricity so cheap that only the rich will burn candles."

The Metric System vs. the U.S. Customary System

The metric system and the U.S. customary system are both systems of measurement. So, what is the difference between them and why are there two different systems? In today's global society, wouldn't it be easier if the whole world used the same system?

Elements of the metric system date back to the reign of Louis XVI in France during the 18th century. In 1791, after the French Revolution, the metric system was adopted by the French as the official system of measurement. The goals of the new metric system were to develop a single unit for physical quantity and to create a measurement system that did not require the use of conversion factors. Specifically, all measurements of length are in meters, measurements of liquid are in liters, and measurements of weight are in grams. All three types of measurement use a common set of prefixes that are related to each other by powers of 10. For example, a decameter is 10 meters, a hectometer is 100 meters, and a kilometer is 1,000 meters. Conversely, a decimeter is 1/10 of a meter, a centimeter is 1/100 of a meter, and millimeter is 1/1000 of a meter. There are no conversion factors required to switch among these different representations of the measurement of length. Time is the only unit of measurement that is not unified by the metric system. Time still requires conversion factors to switch among days, hours, minutes, and seconds.

The U.S. customary system can be traced back to the Roman system of measurement. It is based on the Imperial System, which was used by Great Britain until 1995. Today, the United States is the only country that has not converted to the metric system from the customary system, even though the Omnibus Trade and Competitiveness Act of 1988 stated that the metric system is the preferred system for industry and trade. In the United States, the metric system is most commonly used by the military, medical field, and scientific realms. The customary system is used in most other instances. The customary system measures length in inches, feet, yards, and miles; measures general volume in cubic inches, cubic feet, and cubic yards; measures liquid volume in fluid ounces, cups, pints, quarts, and gallons; and measures weight in ounces, pounds, and tons. The customary system requires conversion factors to convert

Customary System			Metric System		
From	**Multiply by**	**To get**	**From**	**Multiply by**	**To get**
feet	12	inches	kilometers	1000	meters
pounds	16	ounces	grams	1000	milligrams
quarts	4	cups	liters	10	deciliters

Figure 1. Converting units in the customary system vs. the metric system.

units. For example, to convert feet into yards, you must know that there are 3 feet in one yard. You then would divide the total number of feet by three to determine the total number of yards. Similarly, to convert cups into quarts, you have to know that there are 4 cups in a quart.

The chart in Figure 1 shows the conversion factors needed for the customary system compared to conversion of measurement units within the metric system.

Which system do you think is easier?

THE METRIC SYSTEM VS. THE U.S. CUSTOMARY SYSTEM

Consequences and Implications

A3   What are the implications of the United States being the only country that has not officially converted to the metric system? Justify your answer.

_____

_____

_____

_____

_____

Cause and Effect

A2   What caused the French to adopt the metric system after the French Revolution? Support your answer.

_____

_____

_____

_____

_____

Sequencing

A1   List the elements of the metric system and the U.S. customary system in the order in which they were discussed in the text.

_____

_____

_____

_____

_____

_____

Main Idea, Theme, or Concept

C3 Theme: Does the overall theme of the text support the use of the U.S. customary system? Why or why not?

_____

_____

_____

_____

_____

Inference

C2 What inferences can be made from the chart in Figure 1? Support your answer with details from the text.

_____

_____

_____

_____

_____

Literary Elements

C1 Imagine a conversation between an American and a French person about the use of the metric system vs. the customary system. Choose one character from this scenario. Describe your chosen character's point of view on this topic. Use details to support your description.

_____

_____

_____

_____

_____

_____

_____

_____

For Product Safety Concerns and Information, please contact our EU representative: GPSR@taylorandfrancis.com Taylor & Francis Verlag GmbH, Kaufingerstraße 24, 80331 München, Germany.

PGIL2025USA